THE LONG WAY AROUND

RACHEL NORBY

authorHOUSE®

AuthorHouse™
1663 Liberty Drive
Bloomington, IN 47403
www.authorhouse.com
Phone: 1 (800) 839-8640

Unless otherwise indicated, all scripture quotations are from The Holy Bible, English Standard Version® (ESV®). Copyright ©2001 by Crossway Bibles, a division of Good News Publishers. Used by permission. All rights reserved.

Published by AuthorHouse   07/30/2016

ISBN: 978-1-5246-2124-7 (sc)
ISBN: 978-1-5246-2122-3 (hc)
ISBN: 978-1-5246-2123-0 (e)

Library of Congress Control Number: 2016912291

Print information available on the last page.

The Long Way Around
by Rachel Norby

Inspired by a true story

Dedicated to Derek and Kristy,
whose story is a testament to love
and God's faithfulness...

and also to Karlynn and Drew,
who both fought the good fight
and will never be forgotten.

CHAPTER ONE

Brett

"Hey, Johnson, you look tired. Don't stay too late," commented Michelle, one of Brett's colleagues in the math department, as she walked by.

Brett managed a weak smile. "I'll try not to. They wore me out today. I might need a nap when I get home."

It *had* been a long day. Brett sighed as he ran his hand through his hair, so blond it was almost white, looking at the never-ending stack of math assignments that perpetually took over his desk. *Teaching wouldn't be so bad if it weren't for all the grading. And the kids*, Brett thought ruefully. Actually, most of the time, Brett really enjoyed his students. Today had just been one of those days.

He should have had his suspicions before the day even started. It was going to be a full moon that night, and, as any teacher would tell you, the students were always a little crazy on the day of a full moon. He would have laughed at anyone who told him that prior to taking his first teaching job, passing it off as superstition, but after witnessing it firsthand, he really couldn't argue with it any longer. In fact, any change at all seemed to stir up the students, whether it was a full moon, a cold front, a warm front, snow falling, the rumor of snow falling, or just the usual teenage drama that seemed to plague middle schoolers on a daily basis. Junior highers were a breed all of their own, that was for certain.

First hour had started with one of his squirrelly students, Matt, who informed him that he had only had Kool-Aid for breakfast. Matt had raised his hand at least five times that hour, asking questions that were only slightly related to the lesson that day.

Brett had finally had it on the fifth question, when Matt had asked, "Mr. Johnson, why do we always use 'x' as the variable? I mean, wouldn't it be better to use something like 'm' or 'p' sometimes, just to mix it up? Or even better yet, 'k' would be awesome. 'K' as in Kool-Aid!"

Brett had given Matt the official teacher look, which brought a sheepish glance from Matt as he changed his focus to the next problem on his math assignment. He must have gotten the hint because he didn't ask any more questions for the rest of the hour.

Then, right before third hour started, he caught one of his students, Annie, copying her friend's math assignment that was due at the beginning of the hour. He had pulled her aside into the hallway, expressing his deep disappointment in her and informing her that she would receive a zero as well as a discipline referral that would be sent home. Annie had cried and swore she would never, ever do that again. She had pleaded with him not to inform her parents about what happened, but Brett knew that was exactly what was needed. He let her sit in the hall for a bit to compose herself, but she still came back into the classroom with red eyes and a splotchy face.

As the saying goes, "When it rains, it pours," and things continued to decline throughout the day. On his way down to lunch, he had to break up a fight between two eighth-graders whom Brett had thought were friends. It turned out they were fighting over a girl, with one of them claiming the other one had stolen his girlfriend "right from under his nose." Bringing the two to the office to sort out the whole complicated mess occupied over half of Brett's lunch, so he had to quickly scarf down as much of his lunch as he could, forced to save half of it for later.

On his way up from his already hectic lunch, the principal, Mr. Blomquist, had flagged him down in the hallway. "Hello, Mr. Johnson. How are we today?" he had asked.

By "we" Brett knew he had meant "you" and, more specifically, that he needed something. The principal wasn't one for idle chit-chat. Sure enough, Mr. Blomquist followed up with, "So...I know this is short notice and everything, but we desperately need a substitute for fifth hour. Mrs. Anderson went home sick in the middle of the day, and we are short subs. Would you be willing to sub during your prep hour? I wouldn't ask you if I had any other options, but, like I said, we are desperate." He gave Brett the you-will-be-on-my-bad-side-if-you-say-no look.

So what could Brett do but say yes? Though Brett usually preferred not to substitute teach during his only free hour in order to retain some sense of sanity during his day, he felt that he couldn't say no. He had said they were desperate, after all. He forced a smile and said, "Sure, I could do that. No problem," though he knew that the stack of papers would only multiply without time to correct them.

While subbing, Brett was vividly reminded of why he didn't teach seniors. Half of them were into their senior slide mode, their bodies and brains in a comatose state, while another quarter of them were trying to catch up on the weekend's gossip during his lesson. Hey, at least a quarter of them were listening. He hoped.

It was one of those days that he merely hoped to survive. Now, at the end of the day, he felt like one of those semi-conscious senior students he had taught during his prep hour. He simply stared straight ahead at the large mound of papers that he hadn't had time to grade and now had no energy to tackle. *Maybe if I concentrate really hard, the stack will correct itself and enter itself into the grade book,* he thought tiredly. No such luck.

He shifted his eyes from the stack of papers to the picture he had on the right side of his computer desk. A small smile spread to his lips. The mere sight of his wife, Kara, always had the same effect on him. It was almost as if he could feel his blood pressure lower and his heart rate drop. He took a few deep breaths and let the worries of his day slowly seep out of his mind. Though he spent a large part of his day at school, school was not his whole life. That picture always reminded him of that.

Subconsciously avoiding his paperwork, he let his mind reminisce about the first time he had met Kara. It had been in college, at freshman orientation, where the dorm resident directors had put on a carnival for the incoming crew. Brett was in line for the dunk tank with one of his roommates, Preston, whom he had just met that morning. Preston was bragging about how great his arm was and how he was going to hit the lever on the first try. Brett humored him by nodding and smiling, secretly musing how unlikely it was for anyone to hit the lever on the first attempt. As he turned around absentmindedly to take in the surrounding attractions at the carnival, Brett saw a few girls he vaguely recognized as ones he saw moving into the dorm earlier that morning. One of them, a strawberry blonde, smiled shyly at him as he glanced her way. One of her friends stepped forward, introducing herself as Lori, and then gestured to the strawberry blonde, saying, "I'm not sure if you two have met yet, but this is my friend, Kara." Brett and Kara then had chatted a bit while waiting in line, talking about the carnival and their initial thoughts of the campus.

Now, sitting in his chair in his classroom, Brett smiled at how ironic it was that he didn't have any inkling of the fact that the girl standing next to him in line would be his future wife. If truth be told, Brett didn't really feel any sparks fly the first time he met Kara. She was just another face in the crowd on a busy move-in day; one face amongst hundreds that he had seen around campus. It would be almost a full year before the strawberry blonde who occupied the place behind him in line would ever occupy a place in his heart.

Some people talk about love at first sight, but with Brett, it was more like a slow simmer. Like a crockpot set on low, it took a while for Brett to warm up to Kara. She, on the other hand, had her sight set on him from the very beginning, as he would soon find out. He kept seeing her everywhere. Multiple times a day, he saw her walking to or from class while he was going about his daily schedule, and she always smiled and waved at him. In his Old Testament Bible class, she took the seat next to him, and she would often strike up a conversation with Brett before or after class.

Kara wasn't the only one trying to get the two of them together; her roommates were in on the plot, as well. They were all about playing matchmaker. Lori, the outgoing one who had introduced Kara to Brett in line at the campus carnival, headed up the mission personally. Her first real chance came in October, when the college had what it called "Roommate Roulette." This was where people set their roommates up on a blind date with someone else, and everyone went out on a planned outing to some venue. This year it happened to be the Mall of America, and it also happened to be on Friday the 13th.

Strange things happen on Friday the 13th, Brett mused now as he looked back on the whole thing. Lori and Kara's other friends had made a scavenger hunt for them at the Mall of America, which turned out to be a hoot, and Brett had actually had a great time. He still hadn't felt sparks fly when he was with her, but he did think of her as a friend with whom he enjoyed spending time.

Ironically, Brett and Kara didn't start to date until the following year. Brett actually dated someone else the spring of his freshman year, but the two broke up before summer came. During the summer between their freshman and sophomore year, Brett and Kara emailed back and forth, and Brett enjoyed their correspondence, though he still didn't feel any romantic feelings towards her.

During the fall, the two of them started to hang out a little more and really get to know each other better, and it was during this time that Brett began to realize that he looked forward to seeing Kara each time they hung out. He also realized that sometime between his freshman year and his sophomore year, he had begun to find Kara attractive. He wasn't sure when it exactly happened, but it did. By the time the Christmas season rolled around, he couldn't deny that he had feelings for her. The more time he spent with her, the more it affirmed his feelings. The two shared a love for the outdoors, similar values, and a strong belief in God. He was also attracted to her natural beauty; she wasn't done up like a lot of the other girls around campus. With no make-up, her clear complexion shone through. His favorite parts about her physical features were her stunning blue eyes and her hair; it was a thick mane of blonde with just a hint of red that Brett found undeniably attractive. Besides all of this, she had an incredibly humble personality and was very thoughtful, writing Brett little notes to brighten up his day.

Because of all of this, Brett decided that he wanted to date Kara exclusively, so he asked her out on a date for Friday, the 13th of December, which had become a running joke for the two of them, since their initial roommate roulette date was Friday the 13th of the prior year. While out on their date, he took her to a little park overlooking the river, and asked her to be his girlfriend. She, of course, had been waiting for him to ask her for over a year, and she immediately said yes.

The rest is history, Brett thought to himself as he gazed at her picture on the desk. The two dated for a few years, got married immediately following college, and moved to the little town of Mora when Brett got his first teaching job there. After being married for about five years, the two had conceived and were now awaiting the birth of a baby boy. The mere thought of getting to meet his son soon made Brett break out into a huge smile.

Life is good, Brett thought, *even if I have a million papers to correct.* Unfortunately, he had no idea what was soon to come.

CHAPTER TWO

Gina

"You're really coming along well," Gina said to her current physical therapy patient, Josh, as he finished up one of his knee exercises.

Josh gave her a frustrated look. "Thanks, but it's not coming along fast enough for this guy."

Gina smiled sympathetically at him. A lot of her patients felt that way. It always took longer than they thought it should, especially when they were young men, like Josh.

"Well, hopefully you'll get enough range of motion back in your knee to get your next knee surgery done soon," Gina said encouragingly.

"I guess only time will tell," he said as he did his last leg lift.

As Gina gave Josh instructions for his next set of leg exercises, she thought about how he was a unique patient for multiple reasons. For one, he was younger than most of Gina's patients. Many of her patients were senior citizens who had just undergone a hip surgery or something similar, weakened by a combination of age and circumstance. Josh may have been weakened by his initial knee surgery, but he had his youth working in his favor.

Another thing about Josh was that he was determined to push the limits of both pain and time. Where most patients would back off when they felt any twinge of pain, Josh would push past the point of pain to make each session count. Because of that, he had recuperated twice as fast as most of her patients.

Josh also had a unique story that had brought him to Gina's office in the first place. He had torn his PCL, the posterior cruciate ligament, playing baseball the prior summer. The PCL, the ligament deep within one's knee joint, rarely got injured. People more commonly have ACL (anterior cruciate ligament) injuries, but Josh managed to tear his PCL while sliding into second base during a ball game. After his initial surgery, he had gotten an infection in his knee and had undergone a series of antibiotics paired with another knee surgery, which landed him here with Gina at the present moment.

Every week, Josh had been gaining a few more degrees in his knee's range of motion. The doctor wanted his knee to be able to bend at about 130 degrees before he had his next knee surgery, and he was at 90 degrees presently. Though he was gaining quickly, it still seemed painstakingly slow for Josh, as he was expressing now.

"I can't wait for my knee to be back to normal." He rolled his eyes. "If that's even possible after all of this."

Gina gave him a knowing smile. How his knee would heal depended on a variety of factors: genetics, the skill of the surgeon, physical therapy, and his determination to get better. Luckily for him, he had all the factors going in his favor. His family history was a healthy one, he had one of the best knee surgeons in the state, he worked hard in physical therapy, and he was more determined than the average person because he wanted to get back to playing baseball again.

After Josh finished up his last few leg exercises, Gina said, "I'm going to give you a few leg exercises to do at home and send you on your way." She gave him a sympathetic smile, "I know it feels like it has been forever, but you are healing rather quickly, in my opinion. Just keep doing the exercises that I give you, and we'll try to get you back on that ballfield." She handed him some diagrams with explanatory notes. He mumbled a "thank you" and shuffled out the door.

As the door closed behind her patient, Gina meandered back to the desk to finish entering a few notes about the session on the computer. As she sat down, she let out a tired sigh, thinking about the number of patients she still had to see that day. The receptionists had her schedule booked solid the entire day. It made the day go by quickly, but it was a little daunting to look at her schedule in the morning.

When she was done entering notes on the computer, she closed her eyes and took a deep breath to relax herself. She had recently attended a class that emphasized the health benefits of implementing relaxation techniques, such as breathing in deeply and letting it out slowly, so she had made a concerted effort to incorporate a few techniques each day. She wasn't sure if it was helping or not yet, but it felt good to take a breather before tackling the rest of the day.

As she took a few more deep breaths, her mind wandered to her husband, Andy. A small smile played on her lips as she thought of him. In fact, every time she entered the clinic and passed by the lab partition where they tested blood and other things for the patients, she thought of him. The two had met in a lab. While at college in Chicago, the two were in an anatomy class together and wound up as lab partners. Actually, the term "partners" was probably a generous term for the two of them, since Andy ended up doing most of the work in their initial experiment. They were supposed to give lab mice shots of estrogen every six to eight hours around the clock and chart the results. In doing so, Gina was facing two of her biggest fears: mice and needles.

Gina almost laughed out loud as she thought of it now. Andy had agreed to hold each mouse if Gina would do the injections, but Gina kept dropping the needles whenever she got close to the mice. Whether that was due to her fear of mice and needles or because she had realized that she was attracted to Andy, she wasn't sure, but she knew that she was a horrible lab partner. For some reason, he didn't seem to mind. It took a long time to finish the experiment, but the two shared a lot of laughs by the time it was all said and done.

It had almost irritated Gina that she was attracted to Andy. There were quite a few girls at college who made it their mission to find a husband as soon as possible, but Gina had never been like that. She was focused on her studies, and she didn't want a guy to get in the way. Besides that, she was very selective about whom she dated, having a mental list of necessary qualities for a potential spouse, and she would only date if she were extremely serious about a person. Because of that, she hadn't been on a date for quite a while. It wasn't that she hadn't been asked out recently; she had just said no to them because they weren't up to her standards.

She wasn't sure what to do with the nagging sense that she was beginning to like him. She didn't know him well enough to allow herself to cater to her feelings, so it just ended up irritating her. However, she couldn't help but feel a little flattered, as well as intrigued, when he asked her out on a date.

Well, "asked her out" is a relative term when considering how he had gone about it. He didn't actually ask her out face-to-face; he had a much more creative scheme up his sleeve. One day, at the end of

anatomy class, Andy nonchalantly asked Gina if she would fill out a
short survey for him that he would use for one of his classes. He didn't
want her to have to rush to finish it right then, he had explained; he
wanted her to take it back to her dorm room and fill it out when she
had more time.

Later, when she had flopped on her bed for the night, she
remembered the survey and pulled it out. The more questions she
read on the "survey," the more she realized that it wasn't a survey that
had anything to do with school. All of the questions were inquiring
about what kind of date she would like to go on and what activities
she liked to do, ending with this: "If you were to be asked out by the
survey-giver, would you say yes?" She had rolled her eyes, but couldn't
help it as a small giggle escaped from her lips. Would she say yes? That
was a good question.

She had contemplated that very question, tossing and turning
much of the night, until she decided that yes, she would go with
her gut feeling and give him a chance. She didn't know a lot about
him, but she felt like she knew enough to at least give him one date.
The way he had handled the whole mice-needle experiment spoke
volumes about his sense of humor and playful personality, and she
had learned other tidbits about him as the two chatted about their
lives and families over the course of their lab partnership. It was
enough to know that he was a person with strong moral values, a love
of family, and a general love of life, which were three values high on
her list for her future spouse.

The two had gone on their first date in late March. The date was
initially scheduled for a week prior, but Gina had to reschedule due
to a double-booking error on her part. She had previously planned
an outing with her girlfriends, and she wasn't about to break that for
a first date with a guy she had recently met. She had never been the
kind of girl who put guys above her friendships with her girlfriends,
and she wasn't going to start now.

Despite having to reschedule, the two went out and it went far
better than Gina had anticipated. By the end of the evening, which
consisted of dinner and an evening walk, she couldn't deny that she
was beginning to have real feelings for him. Besides the obvious
physical attraction, the two enjoyed many of the same things. They
were both athletic, competitive, had a similar sense of humor, and a

strong faith. One of the things she liked the most was that the two of them laughed a lot together. They both had playful personalities, so every time they were together, the laughter flowed freely.

The date had gone so well that Gina had been surprised when she hadn't received a phone call from him within a few days. Actually, a week after the date, when she still hadn't heard from him, she really started to get worried. She began to wonder if she had only imagined that he had enjoyed the date as much as she did. Even worse was the thought that, after she had finally allowed herself to have some feelings for him, the feelings might not be reciprocated.

However, shortly after that, he did call, and she discovered the reason for his lack of communication. Due to his chronic back pain and his recently swollen neck, Andy had gone to the doctor shortly after their date. The doctors had run some tests, and he had received the news that no person ever wanted to hear: He had cancer. It was right by his kidneys, and he was scheduled to begin cancer treatments soon. He hadn't known how to tell her or what to say, so he just hadn't called for a while.

It had been a lot for Gina to take in. Though they had only been on one official date, she felt like she was invested in the relationship already. Andy had expressed that he would understand if Gina wanted out at this point, since he was unsure of what the outcome of the cancer treatments would be, but Gina was game to keep dating if Andy was willing. He seemed relieved to hear she was still interested, and the two of them continued to date between his bouts of treatments throughout that spring.

When summer arrived, Gina felt more strongly than ever that she wanted to keep seeing Andy. Unfortunately, she would be going out of the country for most of the summer for a mission trip to Ghana, which would make it physically impossible to see much of him. Though it was difficult to leave when Andy was undergoing treatments, she felt like the time away would be a true test of whether or not the relationship was meant to last.

While in Ghana, Gina made a point to pray during her breakfast hour on Andy's chemotherapy days in addition to writing him multiple letters every week. When he called a little over a week into her trip, the sound of his voice invigorated her very being, like a swimmer finally coming up for oxygen. She hadn't realized just how much she missed him until she heard his voice.

Unfortunately, that was all she heard from him during her month-long mission trip. He had promised to write her letters, but day after grueling day working with the impoverished people of Ghana, she never received a single one. She began to imagine the worst. Did he have a change of heart about his feelings for her? Did his cancer take a bad turn and he was physically unable to answer her letters? Both thoughts seemed equally horrifying to Gina.

It was a tough mission trip in more ways than one, so when Gina finally made her way on to the plane to come back to the States, she was physically and emotionally exhausted. She wasn't sure what to expect in regard to her relationship with Andy when she got back, but she didn't have to wonder very long. When she stepped off the plane and made her way to the baggage claim, there he was, waiting for her. The genuine smile on his face wiped away all her fears. He wrapped his arms around her, and as the two pulled apart, he kissed her slowly and tenderly, making all of her questions fade away. She was home, in more ways than one.

Now, looking back, that was the point she knew she wanted to be with Andy forever, however long that happened to be for him. After getting engaged later that year, the two were married the following summer. Though Andy had been in and out of treatment for his cancer during the first five years of their marriage, the two clung to the hope that the cancer would eventually be gone.

That was the hope she was clinging to at the present moment, since now it seemed more important than ever. Despite the uncertainty of Andy's future, the two had decided to start a family. While Andy had been in remission for a stint while they were engaged, the two had decided to bank his sperm just in case they needed it in the future. It was a good thing they had made that decision, since Andy had experienced bouts of cancer ever since then. Gina had then undergone in vitro fertilization in the latter part of last year using the banked sperm, which resulted in her present condition.

Gina looked down and rubbed her enlarged belly, anxiously anticipating the day when she would meet her son. She just hoped he would have a daddy when he came out.

CHAPTER THREE

Brett

It seemed like just yesterday that Brett had held his baby boy in his arms for the first time. *I am the luckiest man in the world,* he had thought, wanting to freeze that moment in time. Never had he felt so close to his wife and to God as he had in that moment.

They had named him Grant, and each time he thought of his name, he thought of how God had granted the two of them such an undeserved gift. Born on May 16th, right on schedule, he was a healthy, happy baby with blue eyes and chubby cheeks that inspired frequent kissing. When his little fingers curled around Brett's, he couldn't help but marvel at what a miracle babies were. Being a teacher of math, it astounded him how many thousands of things had to go right from conception all the way to birth in order for a healthy baby to be born. Each baby was definitely a miracle, and his own personal little miracle never ceased to amaze him.

Kara had beamed the first time she had held baby Grant in her arms, and that same beaming smile had reappeared on her face each time she interacted with him. She loved being a mom and it showed. She reveled in every little movement, every facial expression, every little sound produced by the new addition to the family. Brett loved to watch her with Grant, sometimes even tiptoeing up to the nursery to peek in the room undetected; there was something about the unbreakable bond between a mother and child that left Brett in a constant state of awe.

As the craziness of school ended and summer began, Brett had taken advantage of his time off by spending every possible moment with his wife and son. He and Kara couldn't believe how much Grant changed every week. Sometimes it seemed as if he changed overnight. As the weeks progressed, Grant started putting on more weight, looking around, cooing and smiling (or at least they appeared to be smiles), and becoming more aware of the world around him. Just when Brett thought to himself, *This stage is the most fun yet,* another few weeks would fly by and he would have the same thought about the next stage. Life was good in the Johnson household.

Then, towards the end of the summer, Kara told Brett about some bizarre things that had been happening to her. She seemed rather apprehensive about telling Brett, as she didn't like to complain, but she had finally said, "Honey, I think something might be wrong with me."

Brett had jokingly replied, "Well, yeah, but I still married you," but then he saw the look on her face. His face sobered quickly and he said, "Kara, what is it?"

She had looked down at her hands and said, "I've been really dizzy lately, and not because of being dehydrated or anything like that. I've also had episodes of blurred vision, almost to the point where I have to sit down or I will fall over. I just feel this...bubble-headedness... where it seems like my head is almost physically separated from my body. I can't really describe it in words. It's just been so strange." Her blue eyes met his, and he saw fear in them.

He had grabbed her hand, now visibly concerned as well. "When did this start happening?"

"Well, it started a few weeks ago, but now I have at least one episode of lightheadedness a day, each lasting five seconds or more. At first I thought it was just a passing thing, perhaps something connected to recently having baby Grant, but the more frequently it started happening, the more I began to feel like something was really wrong with me. I'm so scared, Brett. What if something is really wrong with me?"

Brett didn't want to think about the answer to that question, but knew that he couldn't avoid it. The two had decided to go see the doctor to get some answers. When Kara told the doctor about the regularity and severity of the episodes, having started in August and getting more frequent into September, he had recommended that she get an MRI as soon as possible.

After getting the MRI done, the doctor had told them point-blank, "Kara has a brain tumor." The prognosis was bad enough, but what irked Brett was the way in which the doctor delivered the news that no person ever wanted to hear. He had no discernable bedside manner and had just said it matter-of-factly, the way you might tell someone "your shoe is untied" or "your shirt is untucked." It's not like Brett had been expecting the doctor to be in tears or anything, but he thought a little compassion might have helped to lessen the blow a little bit.

Despite the doctor's lack of sympathy, his prognosis was dead-on, and Brett and Kara had gone on to meet with a neurosurgeon at Abbot Hospital. Though the two words "brain tumor" had initially sent ripples of fear through both of them, the neurosurgeon had assured them that there was a good chance the entire tumor could be removed through surgery. He went on to tell them that this brain tumor was in a relatively easy place to remove and that the surgery itself would be rather routine. Seeing that his words were having a calming effect on the two, he added that he had done many surgeries similar to this one and that Kara would be in good hands. "Kara should be in and out of surgery before you know it," he had reassured them.

That was over a month ago. It seemed like just yesterday that Kara had been his perfectly healthy, happy bride and mother to Grant, with Brett feeling like the luckiest man on earth, and now, as he sat in the hospital waiting room while Kara underwent surgery, he wondered if his luck had run out.

A lot could happen in just a few months, Brett thought to himself ruefully. You could become a father, have a wife diagnosed with a brain tumor, and have to wonder if the life you have come to cherish would be ripped out from under you at any moment.

It was so strange to Brett that most people were just going on with their daily routines, unaware that on this particular October day his wife, his precious wife, was undergoing surgery at that precise moment. How many times had he done the same thing, unaware of people's pain around him? How many times had he never given a second thought to the fact that he and his loved ones were alive while other people suffered or died?

Those thoughts haunted him for a few moments, but then they flitted back over to Kara. As he thought about the prospect of seeing his smiling wife again, Brett repeated the reassuring words of the neurosurgeon in his head to calm himself down. *The tumor is in an easy place to remove. It is just a routine surgery. She should be in and out of surgery in no time.* He closed his eyes and sent up a few extra prayers for Kara to be strong and for the surgeon's hands to be swift and skillful. He looked up at the clock and back down at the newspaper that he had been attempting to read over the past few hours. He looked around the room at a few of his family members who had come for moral support; some had legs tapping nervously, some had heads bowed in meditation or prayer, and some sent forced smiles his way as he made eye contact with them. Waiting was always the worst.

Another hour went by and they were still waiting. Kara was scheduled to have been done a while ago. With each passing minute, Brett's anxiety level rose. He tried to stay positive, telling himself that surgeries sometimes went a little longer. *I don't have anything to worry about,* he assured himself. The only problem was that he wasn't very convincing.

Just when he thought he couldn't bear waiting a moment longer, one of the doctors came into the room. After the doctor scanned the room and finally found Brett's eyes, Brett knew something was wrong. Though it was obvious that he was trying to mask it, the fear in his eyes was almost palpable. He cleared his throat and said, "Mr. Johnson, I need to speak with you. Privately."

There are times in life when everything seems to go in slow motion. You feel the individual beats of your heart in your chest and hear each individual breath that you take. This was one of those times.

Everyone's eyes went from the doctor to Brett as he forced his legs to move, following the doctor into a smaller private room. Part of him wanted to hear what the doctor had to say and part of him wanted to run away and hide under a rock somewhere. He raised his eyes and looked expectantly at the doctor.

The doctor cleared his throat, seemingly trying to compose himself before he began. "I am so sorry to inform you that there have been some complications." He paused for a moment, having difficulty continuing.

Brett found his voice, though when he spoke it seemed to have come from somebody else. "What do you mean by complications? I thought this was supposed to be…a routine surgery."

The doctor let out a deep sigh. "It was. The complications have nothing to do with the brain tumor removal."

Brett gave him a confused look. *Nothing to do with the brain tumor removal? What in the world could have gone wrong then?* he wondered.

The doctor continued on. "This might be news to you since we had no knowledge of this from her prior medical history, but Kara appears to have a hole in her heart. Since you didn't inform us of that before the surgery, I am guessing you didn't know about it either." He looked to Brett for confirmation.

Now Brett was really baffled. "A hole in her heart? What do you mean she has a hole in her heart?" Brett's mind switched gears and went a million miles an hour, trying to remember any possible mention of Kara having a hole in her heart from prior conversations with her parents. He could think of nothing. He looked at the doctor blankly.

The doctor gave him a grim look. "We believe she has had this hole in her heart since birth, but it has somehow evaded detection. Usually, if babies have a hole in their heart, it fuses before birth, but Kara's must not have. Prior to surgery, the hole in her heart was relatively insignificant, medically speaking. Many people live their entire lives without knowing they have something like this. However, for this surgery, that piece of information would have been…very helpful to know."

Brett cleared his throat weakly. "What do you mean? Why would that have been so important to know?" He paused and then whispered, "What happened?"

The doctor seemed to be having difficulty determining what to say. "We made a few incisions in Kara's head to remove the tumor. Normally, a little air gets in through incisions and is eventually absorbed by the lungs. However, since Kara had a hole in her heart, the air went through the flap in her heart and straight to her brain." He heaved a heavy sigh and looked away for a moment. "Kara suffered a brain embolism."

Brett didn't know a lot of medical terms, but he knew enough to know that a brain embolism was serious business. He asked the question he had wanted to ask all along but wasn't quite brave enough to voice aloud. "So…is she going to make it?"

The doctor looked Brett straight in the eye. "We're not sure. She has been moved to Critical Care." He paused momentarily. "It's very serious, I'm afraid. She's been placed on life support and is showing very little brain activity. I'm sorry, Mr. Johnson. I wish…it could have gone differently."

Brett was having difficulty processing the magnitude of what the doctor had just told him. *Kara might die? She was on life support? How could that be when she was so vibrant and full of life just that morning?* His mind stumbled through its thoughts.

Then his brain flashed back to the conversation that he and Kara had had on the way to the hospital. Brett had broached the subject of worst case scenarios, in case the worst were to happen. As they approached the hospital, he had cleared his throat, grabbed her hand, and said, "Honey, I know you don't really want to think about this, but what do you want me to do if things don't go well with surgery? Let's say you get put on life support. What would you want me to do?"

Though he had only said it in order to be fully prepared and to know her wishes, she wanted none of it. She had simply said, "That's not going to happen. I don't want to talk about it."

Now he wished they had talked about it. His mind came back to the present and realized that the doctor was waiting for him to say something.

When he finally spoke, it was choppy and illogical. "What… When…Could…I go see her? Now?"

Suddenly, his mind focused and all he could think about was seeing her. For some reason, in the jungle that had overtaken his brain, he thought if he saw her she might miraculously revive. *Those kinds of things happened sometimes, didn't they? The bond of their love could do that, right?* He tried to convince himself that seeing her was all it would take.

The doctor nodded, as if expecting that Brett would ask that. "You may see her soon. She is coming out of surgery and it will be an hour or so until you are able to see her."

Brett anxiously made it through the hour wait and then, after the doctor came back to get him, followed him through a maze of hallways that connected the different wings of the hospital. Everything around him seemed to blur except for the doctor's white coat in front of him.

He stayed focused on that, forcing one foot in front of the other, hoping that he could retain whatever sanity he had left. He needed to be strong for his wife.

They must have been nearing the door to her room because the doctor turned around and leaned towards Brett. When he spoke, his voice was barely above a whisper. "Now, I want you to be prepared. Kara's body has undergone a lot of trauma. Her whole head is bandaged, and some of the bandages may have have traces of blood. In addition, we had to put gauze in her mouth to protect her teeth, as her body is seizing in response to the trauma it has undergone." He took a deep breath and continued. "Also...she will probably be unresponsive no matter what you say or do. I...don't want you to get your hopes up." He raised his eyebrows and gave Brett a firm nod.

Brett didn't know what to think about what the doctor just said. *Don't get my hopes up?* he thought. *All I have left is hope. Doesn't the doctor get that?*

The doctor opened the door, and before Brett entered, he said a silent prayer for strength and, if possible, for a miracle to happen.

On his way in, the nurse on duty was on her way out in order to give him some privacy. She gave him a sympathetic look, and whispered, "I'm so sorry for what you are about to witness. Her body is seizing in reaction to her embolism." She looked back at Kara and then said, somewhat to Brett and somewhat to herself, "That's the body's reaction when it is struggling to stay alive."

When Brett first saw Kara, he couldn't believe how many tubes and IV's were attached to her. She looked extremely pale and fragile, so unlike the strong woman he had grown to love over the years. He slowly walked to her side, grabbing her hand and squeezing it. He half expected her to squeeze his hand back, but as the doctor had warned him, she was completely unresponsive. The doctor whispered something to the nurses in the room, and they subsequently filed out of the room, one at a time, the doctor last, until Brett was left completely alone with his wife. Well, completely alone was not entirely accurate. It was Kara, Brett, and the machine that was keeping his wife alive.

Though he had never really felt at a loss for words around his wife, he felt that way now. What did one say in this situation? Would she be able to hear him? Would she ever be able to hear him again? The thought of his wife never hearing his voice again horrified him.

Whether or not it was true, Brett felt that Kara, somewhere within the recesses of her mind, must be able to hear his voice. He had to at least try.

He squeezed her hand again. "Hey, honey. It's me. The doctor told me about the hole in your heart. It's crazy, isn't it? All this time, it was there inside of you and we never knew it." He paused, looking out the window, gathering his thoughts together.

"The doctors don't seem very hopeful, but I know something they don't." He dropped his voice, whispering conspiratorially. "You're a lot stronger than you look." He cleared his throat. "Plus, we have God on our side. We can't lose, right?" He smiled through intermittent tears.

He sat without speaking for a while, caressing her bandaged face and squeezing her hand. "I love you so much, Kara. I know I should tell you that way more often, so I'm telling you again now." He paused, wrapping both hands around hers. "I need you. Grant needs you. Please come back to us."

He bowed his head, praying for what felt like the hundredth time that day, ending with, "Your will be done. Amen."

As he sat there, contemplating the magnitude of the last words of his prayer, he hoped with all of his heart that God's will would align with his will. He so desperately wanted his wife to live.

CHAPTER FOUR

Gina

Why did everything have to be so difficult? Gina wondered for perhaps the hundredth time as she held Andy's hand at his bedside at their home in Rochester.

Their entire relationship had been plagued with difficulties, but unlike many couples, their problems had nothing to do with each other. Conversely, their plethora of problems could be summed up in one word: cancer. How Gina hated that word. In so many cases, it seemed synonymous with death.

The two had been so hopeful for so long that they would beat this monster that lived inside Andy, but now Gina wasn't so certain. The beast had far-reaching minions to do his dirty work, and Andy's body simply wasn't keeping up with the fight.

As Gina's fingers traced the inside of Andy's palm, her thoughts retraced the past five years, all the way back to when they got married. She remembered how hopeful they had felt then. Andy's initial cancer treatments had been over and his cancer was in remission. The two had their entire lives stretching before them, if only the cancer would stay away.

They weren't that lucky. Just one month after they got married, Andy went in for a check-up. The doctors found cancer again. However, after more tests and having it removed, the cancer was found to be benign. They had both breathed a sigh of relief, hopeful once again that the cancer was a thing of the past.

Andy finished college the following spring, and Kristy started physical therapy school in August. In that same month, Andy went in for another checkup and cancer was found again. However, this time, it was not benign. He would have to do more treatments.

For the next few years, Andy had rounds of radiation and chemotherapy, and the cancer came and went. Gina found it difficult to keep up with the rigor of her physical therapy school while trying to help her husband with all of his medical needs, so she was faced with a difficult decision: Did she stay in school or quit? She had never been a quitter, and she didn't want to start then. On the other hand, was it wise to stay in school when it kept her away from her husband when he needed her most?

In the end, she finished school, with Andy's full support. While getting her diploma, she looked down at Andy, who was seated in the audience, smiling a congratulatory smile, and felt a surge of pride and thankfulness all at the same time for having accomplished something that taken a lot out of both of them.

Gina wasn't the only one who was trying to polish off some academic ambitions at this time. Shortly after she finished physical therapy school, Andy had decided to go to school for prosthetics, a field that interested him immensely. However, after only attending classes for two weeks, the cancer had come back and he was forced to drop out.

This would not be the only time this happened. Andy had started school and dropped out two times due to his cancer treatments. In the end, he simply couldn't keep up with the demands of school while his cancer was coming and going on its own schedule. It was a sad realization for him. Seeing a dream die before your eyes takes a beating on your spirit, which is much more difficult to repair than the body.

Andy's cancer had been on a vicious cycle: Andy would start feeling ill, go in for a check-up, cancer would be found, he would undergo treatments, and then there would be a period of optimism where he felt great and cancer-free for a few months. Then the cycle would rear its ugly head once again.

Shortly after his prosthetic school stint, Andy did something he had never done before: He went to a check-up without informing Gina. He had felt so physically ill that he knew it was going to be really bad news this time, and he wanted to protect Gina from the pain. His gut instinct was correct, and the cancer was so invasive that he would need to receive a bone marrow transplant just to survive.

He did have to eventually tell Gina, and though she was hurt that he had kept his check-up from her, she did understand why he did it. The two needed to focus on his treatments and getting him better, so there wasn't room for holding grudges anyway.

The bone marrow transplant had proven to be the most physically taxing treatment yet. Every day for a month following the transplant, Andy had to have transfusions. His mom and sister switched off staying at the house to help Andy and Gina out. It was a horrible time. Andy was so sick that you could barely categorize him as alive. It made Gina feel almost physically ill herself just watching her husband wilt like a flower without water before her eyes.

It was during this time that Gina, though retaining some sense of hope that he would live, began to face the reality that he more than likely would not make it. She tried to brace herself for the possibility that her son might be born without a father. Though she forced herself to acknowledge that fact, she prevented her mind from dwelling on it. She couldn't afford a mental pity party when there were far more pressing matters at hand.

After being in and out of the hospital, Andy went home with hospice care in early March. If he was going to die, which was becoming more and more of a reality with the doctors giving him only a two percent chance to live, he wanted to be at home with those he loved, not at a hospital with strangers and antiseptic smells all around him.

And now, Gina sat on a chair at his bedside, considering all of this while her husband slept under the close watch of the hospice care nurse. She had lost track of time, mulling over the past five years in her mind. As she continued to trace circles in her husband's hand, his eyelids slowly flickered as he awakened from his long morning nap.

A smile slowly spread across his now-gaunt face. "Hey, Ryp," he said weakly. Gina's maiden name had been Rypkema, so this had always been his nickname for her.

She smiled tenderly at him. She wanted to cherish every waking moment they had together. "Hey, Hammy," she replied, using his nickname in response. "How are you feeling?"

His eyebrows knit together as he considered this. "Not sure yet." He moved his arms and legs a little and grimaced.

"That great, huh?" she said.

He gave her a little shrug. "Yep." His eyes glanced over at the window nearest him and he looked back at his wife. "Would you do me a favor and open it for me?" He loved to hear the birds chirping outside, one of the small joys he had at this point in his deteriorating life.

Gina gave him a sheepish smile. "Sorry, I forgot. I guess I got lost in my thoughts."

She walked over to the window, opening it, and saw some feathered friends on the feeder outside. Their happy chatter made its way through the now-open window and put a smile on Andy's face. He closed his eyes, seemingly relishing in the happiness of the moment.

The two were quiet for a few moments while Gina made her way back to her chair by Andy's bedside. When he opened his eyes, he had more of a serious expression on his face. "How's the little guy?" He reached his hand over and gently placed it on Gina's protruding stomach.

Gina smiled and looked down. "Oh, he's a busy one lately. He's been kicking me all morning." She started rubbing her right side. "He seems to favor my right ribs for some reason."

Andy's eyes were meditative. "I still can't believe we're having a son." He paused for a moment. "Remember back when we first got married and we were seeing that family counselor, Julie? Remember how we talked about wanting to have a kid, cancer and all, and we both felt like God was telling us we would eventually have a son?" He smiled at the thought of it. "It seemed impossible at the time, but look at us now." He gave her a boyishly excited look, though Gina knew he was in a lot of pain.

She couldn't help but smile back at him. His enthusiasm was contagious.

He cleared his throat. "Would you do me another favor?" he asked.

"Sure. Your wish is my command," she said teasingly.

He glanced at his bedside table where his Bible had taken a somewhat permanent residence over the past month. "Would you read to me? Our passages, I mean?"

Gina nodded and reached for the Bible. Each of them had a favorite passage that got them through the hard times. She flipped through the New Testament and found her favorite passage, located in Thessalonians. She cleared her throat and began reading, "First Thessalonians 5:16-18. 'Be joyful always; pray continually; give thanks in all circumstances, for this is God's will for you in Christ Jesus.'" As she looked over at Andy, he was closing his eyes, listening to her voice.

She liked that verse because it continually reminded her to give thanks in all circumstances, even their difficult ones. She had even made somewhat of a game of it; whenever her mind started to drift and think about how tragic life was and how unfair it seemed, she would try to come up with at least three things for which she was thankful. It helped to ward off the "woe is me" pity parties that could easily find a foothold in her thoughts if she allowed it.

He opened his eyes slightly and prodded, "And now mine." He closed his eyes again, waiting for her to continue.

She flipped slightly back in the Bible and found Corinthians. "Second Corinthians 12: 9-10. 'Therefore I will boast all the more gladly about my weaknesses, so that Christ's power may rest on me. That is why, for Christ's sake, I delight in weaknesses, in insults, in hardships, in persecutions, in difficulties. For when I am weak, then I am strong.'" Gina's voice caught on the last line, for she knew Andy was at his weakest point in his life to date.

When Andy heard her voice falter, his eyes snapped open and he reached for her hand. The two sat in silence for a moment, just looking at each other, a silent hug of comfort passing between their eyes.

"I'm so sorry," he said quietly.

Gina forced a smile through eyes that were welling with tears. "For what? Why are you apologizing?"

He heaved a big sigh. "For making you sad. For making everyone sad." His eyes focused back on the window outside. "If you want to know the truth, that's the reason I don't want to die. I hate making people sad. I hate seeing you and everyone we care about cry. I hate..."

His voice began to waver. "I hate the thought that our son could be born without a father and you have to face life alone." He covered his eyes with his hands, breaking down for the first time since he had gotten cancer. A few muffled breaths escaped from him before he continued. "I want to leave a legacy for our son, and the only legacy he will know is death," he said with such tangible pain that Gina couldn't keep her tears from flowing.

As long as she had known Andy, he had been so strong. Even throughout all of his cancer treatments, he had remained optimistic and had made a habit of saying, "Okay, what's next?" Now, seeing him, already physically weakened and gutted by the monster within, emotionally break down was almost too much for her to handle.

She said a silent prayer as the two clung to each other in their sea of pain and misery, their tears expelling years of pent-up grief and anguish.

* * * * * * * * *

Gina and Andy had long talked about what to name their son, since they both felt that names were infused with meaning. They had decided that if Andy lived, their son would be named Samuel, which means "asked of God," since that would indicate that they asked of God and He had granted Andy life. If, in the event that Andy died, the two decided that their son would be named Nathan, which means "gift of God," since he would be a gift no matter what happened.

He was named Nathan.

CHAPTER FIVE

Brett

What do you do when the answer is no? Brett thought to himself as tears rained down his face while he held baby Grant in his arms. He couldn't believe this was happening. Not to him. This kind of stuff only happened to other people or in the movies.

He had always been a very reserved sort of person who liked to prepare for everything, making lists and ensuring that everything was taken care of well in advance. This was not something he prepared for. This was not on the list. This was not part of the Johnson family plan.

After the initial shock of finding out that Kara was on life support, Brett had attempted to sort through the muddled passages of his brain and figure out what he should do. A few things were quite clear.

For one, he knew that Kara's situation was serious. Despite what he had tricked his mind into thinking initially, he had forced his mind to reckon with the fact that she might die. After sitting in the hospital room in Critical Care with her for a few hours, with no response from her no matter what he said or did, mentally digesting the fact that a machine was keeping her alive, not her own body, he realized by himself and for himself that she might not make it.

Also, he knew he had a baby to care for. A baby needed constant care with his never-ending schedule of eating, diaper changes, and taking naps. Moreover, a baby needed love and attention, so Brett knew he couldn't keep Kara on life support forever with a baby who needed him at home. His family had already taken care of little Grant while Brett could sort things out, so much so that he had temporarily forgotten that he even had a baby to begin with. One moment he was sitting there, holding Kara's hand, pleading with her and God that she would live, and another moment he was remembering that he had a life outside the hospital that included his new baby.

A third thing he knew for certain was that God would take care of him no matter what happened. There had been many times in his life, though none as serious as this, where Brett had had a problem and God had been faithful to provide an answer. It might not have always been the answer that he wanted, but there was always an answer. When he was trying to figure out what college to attend, God had been faithful to direct him to Northwestern College, where Brett had always felt academically challenged and spiritually strengthened. When he graduated from college and was looking for a job, Brett found a job in the little town of Mora. When he and Kara had first gotten married and money was tight, they found ways to save money and stretch their hard-earned dollars. When Brett went on a mission trip to the Ukraine with his church and found out he had allergies to the home in which he was staying, God provided the energy Brett needed in the midst of many sleepless nights. When Brett and Kara wanted to have a baby, God had provided a beautiful, healthy baby boy. From experience, Brett knew he had reason to trust, even now when it seemed impossible. That was what it meant to have faith.

After praying for wisdom and seeking the advice of family and friends, had decided to give Kara three more days on life support and then let her go if the situation didn't improve. The Kara he knew loved life and enjoyed sharing it with the people she loved most. The shell of a person on life support in the hospital room wasn't the real Kara. She would never want to live like that, and Brett wouldn't be the one to make her, however desperately he wanted her to live.

Three days. The time went by agonizingly slow, yet Brett felt the impending end of the three days loom over him like a hammer about to fall. Actually, the pressure made him feel like the whole world might implode if he reached the three-day limit and nothing had improved. The pressure came at him from all angles: from himself, from the Life Source people who had been there to gather Kara's organs in case the worst were to happen (Kara had always indicated she was a donor on her driver's license), and from the vacant stares of his family and friends who prayed for the best but feared the worst. He didn't know if he had the strength to carry on like this, yet he didn't know if he possessed the gumption to actually let her go if the time came for that to happen.

Three days. He had cried more in the past three days than he had in his whole lifetime. He couldn't fathom how he hadn't dehydrated yet from the amount of liquid that was pouring out of his body versus the minimal amount that was going into it. In fact, he wouldn't have remembered to eat or drink anything if it hadn't been for his family and friends. They made sure that he was getting regular meals, though he only picked at them anyway. He had lost his appetite the moment Kara had been put on life support.

Three days. His mind processed the events over the past seventy-two hours. At one point, when he had gone out to the car to get something, he had discovered a card from Kara written to him. As Brett slowly took it out of the bag that had never made it into the hospital, it dawned on him that she must have written it sometime shortly before they had gone to the hospital for her surgery and had slipped it into her hospital bag to give to him. Part of him didn't want to open it because of the ensuing pain that would follow, but another part of him wanted to drink in every word that she had to say. She had been alive when she had written this card. Her body and mind were functioning without the help of machines at that point.

As he had carefully opened the card written specifically to him, his eyes, after reading through it all once, had focused on one phrase towards the end of the card: "Don't worry! We will get through this triumphantly!" Despite his heavy heart, he smiled at her optimism. Though he didn't feel very triumphant at that present moment, he had to admire her spirit.

Besides finding the card, another eventful occurrence was the prayer service of his family and friends. Though people were praying around the clock, they had also held a special prayer service for friends and relatives. Though most people kept their prayers to themselves, they all prayed for healing; they all prayed for a miracle to happen.

We all prayed for a miracle that didn't happen, Brett thought to himself now as he held baby Grant in his arms by Kara's bedside, his tears a river down his face, knowing that the three days were up but trying to convince himself that he had more time. Sometimes, God's answer was no, but he was having a difficult time processing why no was the answer in a situation like this. Hadn't he always been faithful in all aspects of his life? Hadn't he always prayed, gone to church, done service work, gone on mission trips, and generally been a good person? Didn't that count for something?

Brett looked at all the machines and then down again at his wife. He couldn't bring himself to say the words that he wanted to say. He tried to choke them out.

He wiped his face and cleared his throat. "Hey, sweetie. It's me again." He paused, collecting his thoughts. He then held the baby up so that, if Kara's eyes had been open, she would have been able to see him. "I have baby Grant here to see you. He misses his momma." The thought of that sentiment and how Grant would forever be missing his mother in the future sent another torrent of tears running down his face.

He coughed again. "We have all been praying. So hard. God must really want you in heaven with him because he didn't bring you back to us." Now the tears were really flowing. He could barely speak anymore.

"Now...now it's time to say goodbye." He put his head down on Kara's chest. "But...it's just so hard." He gripped Kara's hand so tightly that, if she were awake, she would have complained that he was crushing her hand. He didn't want to ever let go.

It was at that moment that his family and friends, who had been waiting in the hallway for Brett to say his final goodbyes, came into the room, silently took baby Grant from him, and surrounded Brett, as if bracing him for what was about to take place. A few of them placed their hands on Brett's back, attempting to give any comfort possible in Kara's final moments on Earth.

After a few minutes and a few forced deep breaths, he raised his head and then slowly lifted his eyes, as if looking up to the heavens. Directly addressing God, Brett said, "Though you are taking her away, I will *never* curse your name."

After a final moment of silence, it was obvious that it was time to go, but Brett couldn't physically find the will to leave Kara. He found himself wondering what his last words had been to Kara before surgery. He couldn't make his brain remember, but he hoped they had been good. Maybe if he imagined himself saying something amazingly romantic and comforting, he could feel some sense of the closure he was seeking.

His family began the procession out of the room, hoping Brett would follow, but in the end, two of Brett's best friends had to carry him down the hall. He simply couldn't bring himself to leave her. Once he left her, it was final. Once he left her, she would be alone with the hospital staff. Once he left her, she was really gone.

Gone. Now Brett felt like he had a hole in his heart to match Kara's. The only difference was that he was fully aware that he had it.

CHAPTER SIX

Gina

He had died. He had actually died. Though the truth had stared Gina in the face for months, she still had a difficult time digesting that it really had happened. It was one thing to *think* that he might die and another thing to actually *see* it happen.

Andy had known and accepted that death was coming. With the exception of his one breakdown, he had had a sense of peace throughout his hospice care. He had tried to make the most of every waking moment, spending time with as many of his friends and family as he could, especially Gina. He made sure to tell each person how much he loved them. In the end, besides his relationship with God, that was what had really mattered.

As he left this earth, he had a vision of the window opening with light pouring out, a sheer curtain fluttering in the breeze as he was welcomed into heaven. It was a peaceful way to leave.

If Andy could have attended his own funeral, he would have seen that he did leave a legacy, just as he had wished. When people spoke at his funeral, even the outsider could have seen how his faith had profoundly affected those around him. Though he would have described himself as an introvert, preferring a few close friendships over a multitude of friends, he had had a deep spiritual walk that was obvious to anyone who came into contact with him. He had always made sure he had his devotional time with God every morning, no matter what was on the agenda for that day. His heart for mission work and helping the less fortunate had also made an impact on those around him.

Andy had died on April 10th, and little Nathan Andrew was born a month and a half later, on May 29th, just one day before what would have been Andy's next birthday. Nathan's birth was bittersweet. While

Gina was so incredibly excited to meet their much-anticipated son, the absence of her husband could be felt in everything. He was not there to drive like a nut to the hospital. He was not there to hold her hand and encourage her during birth. He was not there to hold their son for the first time. He simply was not there, and Gina's heart hurt each time she was reminded of that simple fact.

Despite the hardship of it all, a few seemingly miraculous things had happened that confirmed to Gina that God was still watching out for both of them. For one, the thought of birth had always somewhat terrified Gina, but she had only had sixteen minutes of pain from her water breaking to the time of Nathan's birth. Her aunt, who was staying with her at the time to help her out, had been trying everything to get Gina to go into labor prior to it actually happening, from having her eat spicy foods to exercising to massaging her feet, and the two of them couldn't help but marvel at God's hand in making it all happen so quickly and smoothly.

Another amazing thing that had happened was the sale of their home in Rochester. Immediately following Andy's death, Gina had put their home up for sale. It sold in ten days. Even she couldn't believe it. Some people waited for years to sell their homes, and hers had sold in just ten days.

Immediately following the sale of her home, she had moved in with her parents in Wisconsin so that she could have some help with her new arrival and try to heal emotionally. Her mom and dad were instrumental to her overall sense of well-being during this time. If Gina needed time to just be by herself and cry, which she did often, her parents would take the baby and just give her space. Her mom cooked meals for her and did laundry. They both prayed for her and gave her advice when she asked for it. Gina had always appreciated her parents, but during this time, her filial sentiment was felt more acutely than ever before.

Though the busyness of being a mom forced Gina to function physically, the emotional wound inside of her was still raw and tender. She cried at least once a day, sometimes at unexpected moments. She might be holding little Nathan and rocking him, thinking of how blessed she was to have a healthy son, and she would suddenly notice something wet on her arm and realize she was crying. She might be helping her mom put laundry on the line while the baby slept, and she would abruptly stop, looking into the distance, the pain hitting her like a wave, washing her face with tears. She might be driving and a song would come on the radio that reminded her of Andy and she would have to pull over, unable to ward off the emotional tidal wave that would swiftly overpower her.

Certain dates on the calendar were also difficult, especially the "first" dates right after he died: Andy's birthday that came just one day after Nathan was born; Andy and Gina's first anniversary since his death; driving by their favorite restaurant or favorite park for the first time; attending church and sitting alone for the first time in "their pew"; the first Thanksgiving without Andy; Christmastime without Andy to start some new family traditions with Nate. The dates went by, each hour agonizingly slow as they occurred, and then time would eventually bring another day that would remind Gina that her pain was not a thing of the past but a present process of grief.

To put it simply, Gina felt numb inside. She felt there was almost a physical chasm in her heart that had resulted from Andy's death, and she wasn't sure how it would ever heal. Weren't things supposed to get better with time? Wasn't that what they told people? It had been months, and Gina wasn't sure if her heart would ever heal. Raw pain. That was her reality now.

Though Gina faced pain every day, she made a conscious effort to keep moving forward in her life. Eventually, she moved out of her parents' house into a rental in Superior, still close enough to her parents that they could be over in a jiffy if she needed them. She found what she could only describe as her dream job, a physical therapy position very close to where she lived. Besides that, she found a great daycare for Nathan, so she felt comfortable leaving him while she went to work. Things were falling into place, strangely enough, and Gina's new routine helped her to concentrate on something other than her pain that was always just below the surface.

When Gina found a few moments to sit down each day and think, whether it be when Nathan was napping or if he had gone to bed for the night, she contemplated many things, but one nagging thought always found its way to the forefront of her mind: she didn't want her son to grow up without a daddy. She had always felt strongly that every child did better with a daddy in the picture. A father would give Nathan extra love. A father would provide a firm hand with the future discipline. A father would lead by example. Though she knew logically that all these things were true, she had trouble letting her mind go there because the pain was so still so palpable.

Along with the tension that these thoughts brought her, Gina wondered vaguely if these thoughts were disrespectful to Andy. However, Gina had read somewhere that getting remarried after a death of a spouse did not negate the love or value of the first spouse; it was actually a tribute to the first spouse. If you found the love and companionship so desirable and thus so missed following one's death, then it reflected highly upon the deceased spouse if you eventually remarried. This was the growing sentiment that Gina had as she faced each day alone. She missed Andy more than words could express, but she also wanted to share life with someone again when the time was right. Andy would have wanted that for Gina. In fact, he had even expressed he had wanted that for her before he died.

She began to pray that God would help her find a daddy for Nate. Since she believed strongly in the power of a praying woman, she decided to be specific: She wanted a daddy for Nathan by the time he turned two years old. She knew it was a lot to ask, but she also believed that all things were possible with faith.

She had no idea just how swiftly God would answer that prayer.

CHAPTER SEVEN

Brett

Home. Usually that word made Brett feel a sense of comfort and warmth, but not today. Today it just felt empty.

His family accompanied him on his first trip home after his extended stay at the hospital, for moral support, since they knew that stepping into the home where he and Kara had made so many memories was going to be extremely difficult for him. They waited outside and gave Brett the time and space to enter on his own accord, baby Grant in tote.

Before he even entered the house, he noticed that the landscaping job that he had started prior to Kara's surgery was now complete. Some of his friends from church had taken it upon themselves to do something tangible to show Brett that they cared about him, and they had done a beautiful job. Lining some steps that came up from the grass were large rocks on top of a plastic ground cover, with various hostas and other flowers interspersed to give the landscaping a rock garden sort of look. He smiled a grateful smile, his eyes tearing up at the thought that Kara would have loved to see it. She had always loved flowers and spending time outside, and this landscaping job would have most definitely encouraged some spontaneous outdoor time. Brett was so thankful to have such supportive friends. Besides God and his family, his friends were what had kept him standing upright, sometimes literally, over the past week.

As he approached his blue two-level home, he turned the knob and pushed the door open slowly. The door creaked a little, reminding Brett that he had been meaning to oil the hinges for a few weeks now. It was odd for him to consider the fact that he would be doing the normal, mundane household tasks once again, whether Kara was there or not. Life would go on, even without her there. It didn't really seem possible, but time kept its perpetual marching to a steady rhythm of seconds, minutes, and hours no matter what occurred each day.

After opening the door, he entered their kitchen. Immediately, a flood of memories washed over him. He pictured Kara cooking at their stovetop, underneath their newly-remodeled cupboards, making something wholesome and delicious. He pictured her setting the table and making idle chit-chat as she worked. He pictured the two of them sitting down together, discussing what had gone on that day, laughing at various moments, enjoying each other's company. Those normal, inconsequential things had happened nearly every day in this very room, and he had never considered how meaningful they were. Before, it was just dinner. Now, it seemed like something just short of heaven if he could have Kara there doing those simple things once again.

His eyes, after taking in the stovetop, shifted to the refrigerator, where they had multiple family pictures. There was one in particular that immediately grabbed his attention. There was a photo of Kara and baby Grant that had just recently been put on the fridge. Kara was looking down at Grant, a huge smile on her face, her strawberry-blonde hair cascading over her shoulders. Just the sight of her hair made Brett subconsciously reach out to touch the photo, wishing all the while that she were the real thing instead of just a picture. *Oh, how I will miss that beautiful reddish-blonde mane of hair*, he thought to himself as a solitary tear rolled down his cheek.

He wiped the teardrop from his cheek and forced his eyes away from the photo, turning his attention to the next room, the family room. There were various baby toys and accessories around the room, but his eyes immediately focused on the couch. As with much of their furniture, they had gotten the couch second-hand, trying to save money, but it had always felt like "their couch" anyway. For some reason, just the sight of the couch expelled multiple tears from his eyes. How many times had the two of them sat at that couch? How many times had the two of them popped a batch of popcorn, watching a movie or some outdoor show on the television, cuddled up in a blanket and just enjoying each other's company? Now, he would be sitting alone at the couch.

Brett let out a deep sigh and forced his legs to go towards their bedroom. This room would be the hardest of all, and he knew it. As he went through the doorway, he immediately saw all of the photos of the two of them that Kara had so meticulously updated and arranged around the room.

There was one of their wedding day, the two of them holding hands and smiling, excited to spend the rest of their lives together. He was glad they didn't know then how short that would be, since that would have put a damper on the day. *Maybe it's a good thing none of us know how many days we have left,* Brett reflected.

There was another photo of a vacation the two had taken. When some people say the word "vacation," they envision sandy beaches and endless blue waters. Not Brett and Kara. The two of them loved camping and spending time outdoors. A perfect vacation to them was heading up north, canoeing and fishing in the many lakes that Minnesota had to offer, and cuddling together in the tent after an adventurous day outside. Those kinds of vacations were inexpensive, easy to plan, and encouraged a lot of together time. In this particular picture, Kara was holding up a fish that she had caught, and Brett had his arm around her, smiling at the notion that his wife had just out-fished him. Just looking at the photo put a smile on Brett's face now, tears splashing over the corners of his smile.

One of the last large mounted photos in the room was a recent picture of the two of them with the new arrival. Kara was looking down at the baby and Brett was looking at Kara. One of their parents had snapped the picture, and the two of them had liked it so much that Kara had added it to their bedroom menagerie. Brett reflected on the picture itself. He hadn't taken the time to really notice it before, but now, in a more contemplative state of mind, he found it ironic that he was looking at Kara instead of at the camera. He had always enjoyed watching Kara interact with Grant, and the picture exemplified that fact. *What I wouldn't give to have just a few minutes right now of watching Kara with Grant,* he thought ruefully as he let his eyes linger on the photo.

After gazing at the remainder of the photographs, his eyes moved on to their bed. Instantly, an almost tangible palpation of pain hit his stomach and made him feel queasy. Their bed. So many memories. Of course, there were the obvious, those of cuddling and romance, but, moreover, he remembered other moments. He remembered coming into the room while Kara was napping, the intermittent rays of sunlight reflecting off of her strawberry blonde hair, as peaceful as a baby sleeping. He remembered the anticipation of baby Grant, with Kara getting larger every week and Brett putting his hands on her stomach to feel the baby kicking. He remembered the painful times, too, especially shortly after Kara had received her prognosis of having a brain tumor and Brett had held her, crying, against his chest on multiple nights.

As he reminisced on all of those memories, he wasn't sure how he was going to be able to sleep on that bed that night, all alone for the first time. In fact, he wasn't sure how he was going to do anything anymore. *Alone.* As he weakly sat on the bed, the full impact of that word hit him. She was gone. He was alone.

He suddenly looked down and remembered that he had baby Grant in his arms. Grant had been so quiet throughout Brett's meandering through the house, he had almost completely forgotten he was there. Just the sight of the baby reminded him that he wasn't alone. Grant smiled up at him, as if to say, "Daddy, you're not alone. We're in this together."

Brett smiled back. Then, out of the corner of his eye, he noticed something on the bedside table. A Bible was there, just underneath the lamp for nighttime reading. It was the one that Kara had been reading shortly before she went into surgery. As he glanced at it, he was reminded that he really wasn't alone after all. God was there. Even when he didn't feel it.

CHAPTER EIGHT

Gina

The days were getting a little easier as time went on, but not much. In a conversation during one of his last stays in the hospital when death was seeming like more of a possibility, Andy had told Gina, "Time will heal, but there will always be a scar." He couldn't have been more accurate in his description. Gina was healing, slowly, but the scar of what had happened would always be there, reminding her of what she had lost.

Strangely enough, when Andy died, the knowledge that he was finally cancer-free and enjoying his perpetual health in heaven had lifted a weight from Gina's chest that she could physically feel. It was as if she had had the cancer too, and as it had invaded Andy's body, it had done the same inside of her. Then, at Andy's death, when his physical body was laid to rest, she felt the weight of the cancer lift from her body as well. The only problem was that the weight of his illness may have lifted, but the hole left in the wake of his absence could not be filled so easily.

Since Gina had been praying for a daddy for Nate by the time he was two, she figured she should probably make an effort to enter the dating world once again. However, if she was being completely honest, she really felt at a loss as to how to begin that whole process. For one, she never planned on having to begin a relationship again, so she was a little out of practice. Another thing was that she had never been the flirtatious type, and she wasn't about to start now. She still wore her wedding ring from Andy and didn't plan on taking that off any time soon, which was obviously a deterrent to prospective dates. She also had no idea where to look for available men, since she didn't want to meet men at bars or go out partying at night. The only places she really went were to work and to church, and she couldn't think of any available men at either place who would even remotely interest her.

She didn't have to wonder too long about the whole reentry into the dating world because a blast from her past contacted her. John, one her male friends from college, emailed her to express his sadness after hearing about Andy's death and his desire to help in any way he could. The two emailed back and forth for a while, and he suggested that they meet for dinner so that they could talk in person. Though she wasn't sure how she felt about it, she decided she would meet him. *Why not? It couldn't hurt anything, could it?* she asked herself.

The two agreed to meet at a Chinese restaurant located midway between their home cities. Gina had always loved Chinese, so she figured that even if the date was a bust, she would at least get a good meal out of it.

As she was driving to the restaurant, Gina's mind churned along with her stomach. *What am I getting myself into?* she wondered. *Am I really ready for this?*

Though she had been friends with John in college, she had never considered dating him before. As she drove down the interstate, she tried to recall the reason for that. She remembered that she had always found John attractive with his athletic build and his charming smile, but she knew it took a lot more than an appealing physical appearance to win her over. She also recollected that she had always enjoyed hanging out with him and their group of friends; John's fun-loving personality and ever-present sense of humor had made him well-liked by most people on campus. She racked her brain, but could not pinpoint the exact reason why the two had never dated before.

She then began to wonder about his life. *Has he been dating recently? What is he looking for in a girl? Has he changed since college? Have I changed since college? Will we even be compatible?*

She began to get annoyed at herself. Her thoughts were incredibly girly and emotional, two adjectives that usually did not apply to her. *Oh well*, she thought. *I guess I'll have all of my questions answered soon.*

She saw the sign for the Chinese restaurant up ahead on the right. After switching lanes and turning, she found a parking spot right by the front of the restaurant. She took a few deep breaths, both to calm herself and attempt to invigorate herself with some last-minute courage, opened the car door, and walked towards the restaurant.

When Gina walked in the door, a Chinese woman greeted her at the front table and asked her how many were in her party. Gina gave the woman her name and told her that she needed a table for two, but wasn't sure if the gentleman she was meeting had arrived or not. She politely asked if she could look around, and after she did a quick scan of the restaurant, realized he was not there yet. Gina looked at her watch and realized that she was five minutes early, so she may as well just get the table and wait.

The hostess showed her to a small booth tucked away into the corner of the restaurant where Gina would be able to see John when he entered the front doors. She glanced around at the décor, and though the restaurant was clean and tidy, the walls and surroundings looked as if they needed a bit of an update. Just being inside a restaurant made her realize how she hadn't been out to eat in a long time. Her life had consisted of taking care of Nathan, working, getting stuff done around the house she was renting, and trying to get as much sleep as possible in order to face each day with at least some semblance of a rested body. She didn't have much money or time left over for eating out.

A movement in her peripheral vision brought her mind back to reality, and she saw John stride through the restaurant doors. After looking around the restaurant, he saw Gina wave from the corner, and, after informing the hostess that his date was already inside, made his way over to her.

Gina stood up to greet him, but realized awkwardly that she wasn't exactly sure what kind of a greeting was suitable in this situation. A handshake would seem too businesslike, but a hug would seem too personal for someone she hadn't seen in years. She settled for a smile and a hello, and he returned the smile readily.

After he gestured for her to be seated first, he sat down on the other side of the booth. To break the ice, he asked, "How was your drive?"

She thought about it a moment before answering, and then said, "Actually, it was nice. I was enjoying the sunshine and the cool breeze that was coming through my windows." After pausing a moment, she added conspiratorially, "I prefer having the windows down over air conditioning. So if my hair is a little crazy, it's because the wind was going through my hair the entire way here."

He smiled, seemingly amused by her last comment. "I like the wild-haired look. It's a bit more natural than all of those ladies who slick their hair down and worry about one hair going out of place."

She rolled her eyes. "Oh, I am definitely not one of those types of girls. You don't need to worry about that."

He leaned back in the booth and crossed his arms as if assessing her. "I seem to remember that about you. You never really fretted too much about your appearance or what anyone else ever thought about you." His eyes twinkled. "I like that in a woman. I've dated too many of the other kind, I'm afraid."

After a bit more small talk, the two ordered their meals and talked for quite a while. The conversation flowed quite easily between the two of them, and Gina found herself having quite a good time with John. He told some stories from college and the two reminisced about old times, laughing pretty heartily about a few of them. The Chinese food was also rather good, and by the end of their meal, Gina found herself feeling glad that she came.

After the two said their goodbyes, John had asked if he could call again, and Gina agreed. *What could it hurt?* she thought to herself as she approached her car. *I definitely had a good time, and I may as well do it again. I need a little distraction in my life right now. At least I'm not thinking about how much I hurt right now,* a small part of her said.

After getting into the car and heading home, she replayed the evening in her head. Though she had enjoyed herself that evening, she still felt that there was something about John that had kept her from dating him in college, but she still couldn't pinpoint what it was.

She listened to a few songs on the radio, and then it suddenly hit her. John had always been a great conversationalist and one who could make her laugh with his ready sense of humor, but he never went deeper than surface level. That's what had always made her keep her distance from him. That was also what she suspected had kept other ladies from marrying him. As her mind replayed the evening again, she recounted that all of their conversation had been about the lighter things in life, like their jobs, the weather, college memories, and things like that. Not once had the conversation gone deeper than that.

Now Gina felt a little torn. She had agreed to a second date, and she would keep her word on that. She just hoped that perhaps the light conversation was due to the fact that it was a first date and not because he hadn't changed much since college. Only time would tell.

CHAPTER NINE

Brett

*H*ow? That was the big question that continually went through Brett's head as he attempted to function each day.

Most people probably would have been asking themselves the "Why me?" kinds of questions, such as "Why did God let this happen to me?" or "Why did she have to die?" Not Brett. He was more concerned with the "how" questions. *How will I make it through each day? How will I take care of baby Grant? How will I ever be able to feel joy again? Those* were the kinds of questions that plagued him during the day and haunted his thoughts at night.

Night. That was the time where his mind played tricks on him, beginning with the moment he walked into the bedroom. When he shut the lights off, physically unable to see but mentally able to imagine, he could almost convince himself that Kara was there with him just on the other side of the bed. A few times he had actually rolled over and tried to put his arm around what he imagined to be Kara, only to be met with cold bed sheets. Though exhausted from work and taking care of a baby, his mind would not shut off at night. Sometimes he would recall a special moment he had with Kara, like cuddling under the stars while camping together, and other times his mind would relive the horror of the last few days she had on Earth. This turned him into somewhat of a functional insomniac, yearning for that elusive good night's sleep.

Despite his lack of sleep, Brett did survive each day by taking one day at a time and relying on the strength transferred to him by God and his friends. Brett, though emotionally more wounded than ever before, felt God's presence more strongly than he had ever before. It was as though God was speaking directly to his situation each time he opened up his Bible. And though neither his family nor Kara's lived in Mora, Brett had plenty of support from his friends from both school and church. A tight group of his guy friends, some of whom had been with him during Kara's final moments, called and stopped by regularly to make sure that he was surviving. He received a torrent of cards and letters, both from friends and from acquaintances, expressing their sorrow at what had happened and offering encouragement. People stopped by with ready-made meals so that he wouldn't have to cook on top of all of life's other pressures. His colleagues from school even took a collection to pay for house-cleaning services for a whole year.

Brett was fully aware that some of the encouragement that took place could only happen in a small town like Mora. *You have to love small towns,* Brett reflected. Everyone knew everyone, which could be both a blessing and curse at times. Though he appreciated all of the heart-felt visits, cards, and homemade goodies, he did not always feel the same appreciation for some people's well-intentioned but often misplaced comments. One comment that totally irked him was when people said, "This was NOT God's will for you." *Really?* he thought. *How do you know God's will? Can you speak for God?* Another comment that frustrated him was, "Don't worry. There's someone else out there for you." As if that's what he was really worried about at the present moment. "Let me grieve before you talk about finding someone else!" he wanted to shout at them, but was always too polite to do so.

Though the cards, visits, and general outpouring of kindness from others helped ease the pain in some way, Brett began to feel the need to talk to someone else who had been through a similar situation. For some reason, he felt like it would mean more coming from someone who had actually walked down a similar road as he had rather than all the people who could only *imagine* what it would be like to be in his shoes.

As he probed his mind, he recalled a family from his church, the Simonson's, who had suffered through tragedy similar to his. He closed his eyes and tried to remember what exactly had happened, and then it came to him. The husband had lost his first wife in a terrible drowning accident after she had attempted to clear snow off of the family skating pond, fallen through, and gotten trapped underwater. The wife had lost her first husband due to an illness that had finally conquered his world-weary body, leaving her with multiple children to take care of on her own.

The more he thought about it, the more strongly he felt the need to contact them and at least have one conversation with them. Just the thought of having someone else who understood, who really understood what he was going through, made him feel a sense of hope within that he hadn't felt since Kara's death.

What he couldn't know at that time was that there was someone else out there who had been through the exact situation that he had and was looking for the same thing: someone who could truly understand and help heal the hole within.

CHAPTER TEN

Gina

"Mom," Gina said, rolling her eyes. "It's just hard to explain in words."

Gina was over at her parents' house in Wisconsin for a visit, and she was in the middle of telling her mom about John.

Her mom smiled and looked at her. "You said he was good-looking, right?"

"Yes." Another eye roll.

"And funny?"

"Yes." A big sigh.

"He's a Christian?"

"Yes. Mom, we've already been over this," Gina said in an uncharacteristic whine.

"And successful?"

"YES!"

Now it was her mom's turn to roll her eyes. "Then what's the problem?"

Gina put her hands on her face and buried her head into the pillow on the couch. "I don't know," came the muffled reply.

Her mom came and sat down on the couch beside her and rubbed her back. Gina relaxed her muscles as she felt her mom's fingers roll up and down her spine.

Gently, her mom said, "I'm not trying to play matchmaker or anything here. I'm just trying to understand what you're telling me."

Gina finally sat up and looked miserably ahead of her at the blue wall on the other side of the room. "It's hard to explain exactly what it is, Mom. I just know he isn't right for me."

Her mom gave her a sympathetic look. "Well, you told me about your first date and how you had fun, but felt something was a little off. What happened on the second date?"

Gina turned and looked at her mom. "We went out to eat at a diner and had hamburgers and malts."

Her mom raised her eyebrows. "Hamburgers and malts? You love hamburgers and malts."

Gina sighed. "I know. But that was the best part of the date."

Her mom stifled a giggle. "And what did you two talk about?"

Gina's brow was knit in a confused look. "I think the better question to ask is maybe what we DIDN'T talk about. And the answer would be 'anything personal.' I think that's the problem."

Now her mom looked a little perplexed. "What do you mean?"

"Well, we have lots of fun together, but we only talk about surface-level things. Like what we did during the week. The weather. Our jobs. Things we like. That's it. We never went deeper than that."

"Maybe he's trying to be sensitive about your situation right now and doesn't want to ask you any personal questions that might upset you," her mom offered.

Gina considered this. "That's what I thought initially. But then I remembered that the reason the two of us never dated in college was because of that very thing. He was super fun, but there wasn't any depth there."

Now her mom looked ahead miserably. "Hmm. Well, we can't have that, can we?"

Gina leaned her head on one hand. "No."

Her mom all of a sudden snapped her fingers. "Hey! I just remembered that there was something that I have been meaning to tell you!"

"Geez, Mom. You almost gave me a heart attack snapping in my face. What is it?"

Her mom gave her a sheepish smile. "Sorry about the snapping." She cleared her throat. "Well, you know how we all used to live in Mora before we moved to Wisconsin?"

Gina nodded. Of course she remembered. They had lived there for a while.

"Well, there is a guy who lives there named Brett. Brett Johnson." She paused, waiting for Gina's reaction, as if the name was supposed to ring a bell.

Gina gave her mom a look. "Yeah? What about him? There are a million Johnsons in every Minnesota town, Mom. I honestly don't remember a 'Brett Johnson' at all."

Her mom looked up, as if thinking. "Actually, I think he may have moved to Mora after we left. So I guess you wouldn't remember him." She was quiet for a few moments, still lost in thought.

"And?" Gina prodded.

"Oh. Right. Sorry." She smiled at her daughter apologetically. "Anyway, I still have a lot of friends in Mora, and one of them, well, you know Mary, of course, told me that this Brett Johnson's wife just passed away during a surgery and that he has a young son the same age as Nathan. He has been having a tough time, too." Her mom paused and looked straight at Gina. "Well, I was thinking. Maybe you should contact Brett."

She looked at her mom skeptically. "Contact him? What do you mean by 'contact him'? You want me to ask a guy I don't even know on a date or something?"

Her mom gave her an exasperated look. "No, no. All I mean is that you should introduce yourself and tell your story. You two have such similar circumstances and you both could use someone who understands what the other has gone through. Offer each other some encouragement."

Gina sighed. "I suppose we could all use some encouragement. And it would be nice to talk to someone who understands exactly what I am going through."

Her mom offered an understanding smile. "Exactly. Plus, what's the worst that could happen? You two talk to each other a bit, and, in the process, discover someone who can understand your situation. Maybe you simply become friends who can encourage each other. What's wrong with that?"

Gina looked off to the side, considering what her mom said. After a few moments, she said, "Well, I'll think about it."

Her mom patted her on the leg and went back into the kitchen to finish cooking lunch. Gina let out a small sigh and added so quietly that her mom couldn't hear her, "I guess it couldn't hurt anything."

CHAPTER ELEVEN

Brett

Since Brett had resolved to contact the Simonson's, he had conversed with them twice, and both times had been extremely insightful.

The first time was over the phone, which was a little awkward at first, but then it had blossomed into a flow-into-the-next-topic-without-thinking kind of conversation. It had seemed amazing to him that Kathy, the wife with whom he had spoken, had been through the same gamut of emotions that he had: shock, emptiness, feeling overwhelmed, frustration, extreme exhaustion, but at the same time a sense of encouragement, love, and hope for a future. She even had cried a little on the phone, still mourning the loss of her first spouse who had left this earth far earlier than she had anticipated. She had apologized sheepishly for her tears, which she felt were silly when she was trying to offer him encouragement, but Brett reassured her that her tears actually helped him to understand that, even if he happened to marry again one day, he would always be mourning the loss of his first love.

Since Kathy's husband, Al, hadn't been home at the time, she ended the conversation with an invitation for Brett to come over for dinner sometime soon when Al would be there. Brett had readily agreed, and the two had set the date for the following Saturday.

Brett had looked forward to the dinner all week for multiple reasons. For one thing, he missed having the company of someone at dinner with whom he could actually converse. He loved baby Grant, but a six-month old couldn't exactly carry on a good dinner conversation. Or any conversation at all. Most of the words exchanged during dinner were something along the lines of, "Did you like that, buddy?" referring to one of the many kinds of baby food Brett had been experimenting on Grant lately.

Another reason Brett had been looking forward to the evening was because he simply loved a good, home-cooked meal. He had been receiving some meals here and there from friends in town who dropped them off on a rotating schedule, but there was something about the taste of food that just comes out of the oven and melts in your mouth upon entry. Though he was a decent cook, it had been Kara who had done the majority of the cooking in their household.

The last reason he had been looking forward to the dinner was because he truly felt that having a conversation with both Al and Kathy together would be a pivotal moment in his healing process. He felt strongly that he needed to speak personally to people who really understood what he was going through at that point in time.

Saturday had come and gone, and Brett couldn't believe how well the evening had gone. Dinner, a beef roast from one of Al and Kathy's steers on the dairy farm, sided with potatoes, onions, carrots, gravy, and fresh bread, had been absolutely delicious. The dinner conversation had been a pleasant one that consisted of getting to know each other better, since they had all gone to church together for years but never really had a chance to really sit down and talk. Then after dinner, the three had sat down in front of the fireplace with apple pie dessert and started talking about deeper things, like how Brett was doing and what he could expect to feel coming up. There were tears shed on both sides, but they were cathartic tears and helped to partially mend the hole Brett had felt on the inside for the past month.

After Brett had gotten home, he had decided to grab the mail on his way in. He set it on the table and then talked for a few minutes with his babysitter, Jill, who was one of the girls at school whom he had taught in math class. She had babysat a couple of times for Grant, and he really seemed to take a liking to her, which made leaving Grant a lot easier for Brett.

Jill had given him the low-down on the evening, finishing with a humorous story about how Grant had attempted to sit up on his own multiple times after she had sat him down on the ground, but wasn't strong enough and kept tipping over. The last time he tipped over, he had rolled around onto his back and just lay there as if saying, "I surrender. I just can't do it." Jill giggled as she finished her story, and Brett joined in, mentally picturing Grant tipping over.

Brett paid her for sitting and she left, and Brett was left staring at the pile of mail on the table. He decided to go through it, since he knew his mind wouldn't shut off enough to go to sleep with his recent conversation with the Simonson's bouncing around in his head.

After tabbing through multiple bills, he came to a handwritten envelope addressed to him. He paused and looked at the return address, and he didn't recognize the name on it or the address. *Oldham*. That didn't ring a bell. Curious, he decided to open it and see who this Oldham person was.

The letter was written personally to him, and he flipped to the very end and saw the full name of Gina Oldham. He searched his mind for any trace of recognition and found none. He decided to read the whole letter and see if it helped to ring a bell at all.

Brett,

My name is Gina Rypkema-Oldham, and I grew up in Mora. I'm so sorry about the loss of your wife. I lost my husband in April to cancer, so I understand your loss. I also have a son, and he is five months old now. He has been a joy and such a special piece of my husband to have.

Life was so hard the first few weeks after Andy died. I missed holding his hand, lying in bed next to him, and talking to someone at night - I still miss those things, but the pain has eased. At first the hole seems so huge and deep, it's hard to imagine that you can move on - but you can and eventually you will. I have found so much comfort knowing that Andy is now in the arms of Jesus and that he is not suffering anymore. I realized that Andy is the lucky one; he got to go to Jesus so soon.

After he died I felt like my dreams and hopes for the future had all disappeared, but slowly God has been giving me a vision for what he has for me in the future. Although we may want to ask the question, "Why, God?" the question we should be asking is, "Who is God?"

God is there for you. He has a plan for you and your son. God loves you so much, and you can depend on

God to provide for you. God will help you raise your son. You will find joy in life again and will laugh again. Life will be different, but it can still be good. Take the time you need to grieve - it's okay to cry and cry often. Don't rush ahead, but don't let yourself get stuck in a rut, either. You can make it through this.

I'm so sorry that another person has to go through what I have. It's so painful, but maybe it will help you to know that there is someone else out there who understands how you feel and has been where you are - and can honestly tell you that you'll get through this.

Gina Oldham

P.S. II Corinthians 1:3-7 verse says, "For just as the suffering of Christ flows over into our lives, so also through Christ our comfort overflows." Hope that helps!

Wow. Brett didn't even know what to think after reading that. Here he had just gotten back from conversing with a couple who had been through a similar situation, and now he had a letter from a young lady who was dealing with exactly what he was dealing with right now. *Now.* That was the key word.

His heart almost physically felt the encouragement offered by her words. "You can make it through this. You will make it through this," the letter had said. Brett repeated those words over and over to himself as he considered this unique woman who had taken time out of her own busy life and her own grieving to encourage him.

He decided that the least he could do was write her a letter back. She deserved to know how much her letter had touched him and encouraged him. Maybe he could offer a little of the same to her. Maybe he could help ease her pain the same way she had eased his. Just maybe.

What could it hurt? Brett thought to himself as he pulled out a piece of paper and a pen.

CHAPTER TWELVE

Gina

*F*inally, Gina thought to herself. *Nap time for little Nathan.* She loved her son, but she also relished his nap time when she had the chance to catch up on some household chores, contact friends, or just sit down to relax for a few minutes.

Being a single mom could be exhausting, but she was so grateful that she had Nathan in her life. She couldn't imagine life without him. He had given her a sense of purpose following Andy's death, a time when she felt like curling up into a ball and just sleeping the day away to block out the pain. Instead, she had a son to take care of and that forced Gina to act. He also got Gina to smile, albeit through salty tears at times. He was her one piece of Andy that she could invest love and energy into every day. He was her reminder of life.

Gina picked up some of Nathan's toys in the living room and then decided to check her mailbox, hoping for something other than bills. It was always nice to get something personal in the mail. She was fortunate enough to have been receiving a lot of cards and letters over the past six months from family and friends, and that had helped immensely with the emptiness and loneliness. It reminded her that she was not alone and that she was loved.

She pulled out a stack of mail and started sorting through it. Though she put quite a few in the bill pile, she did get three letters. She always opened those first. Bills could always wait.

The first one was from her mother. She smiled. Her mom sent her one note every week without fail. Sometimes she enclosed coupons for diapers or other baby supplies, and sometimes she sent an easy recipe that Gina could prepare in a short amount of time. Other times she just sent a note with encouraging quotes or Bible verses. She counted herself blessed to have such a supportive mother.

She flipped to the second envelope and saw that it was from her good friend, Allie. Allie had the knack of always being able to make her laugh, no matter what mood Gina was in. She was excited to read that letter.

She tabbed through to the last note and saw the return address was from Brett Johnson. *Hmmm,* she thought to herself, *he did write back.* After making the instant decision to open his letter first out of the three, she flipped to the other side of the envelope and saw a little "P.S." note that was written in all capital letters. It said:

SORRY IT TOOK SO LONG FOR ME TO REPLY. I WROTE YOU A NOTE SHORTLY AFTER RECEIVING YOURS, BUT YOU MUST HAVE PUT YOUR FORMER MORA ADDRESS ON THE RETURN ADDRESS LINE BECAUSE IT WAS SENT BACK TO ME. I HAD TO TRACK DOWN YOUR CURRENT ADDRESS AND IT TOOK SOME TIME (LONG STORY).

Oh no! she thought to herself. *How embarrassing! What a great first impression I must have made.* She silently chided herself for her mental slip. *Well, I guess he was willing to track down my current address, so he couldn't have been that annoyed at me.* She decided to open up the letter to see what this Brett had to say.

GINA,

TO BEGIN WITH, I WANT TO THANK YOU FOR THE VERY THOUGHTFUL CARD AND PERSONAL NOTE YOU SENT TO ME. HOWEVER, MOST IMPORTANTLY, I TOO WANT TO EXTEND MY CONDOLENCES TO YOU AND YOUR SON FOR YOUR LOSS. MY HOPE IS THAT YOU HAVE FELT THE LORD'S PRESENCE AND STRENGTH AS I HAVE. ALTHOUGH I HAVE BEEN A CHRISTIAN SINCE I WAS A KID, I HAVE NEVER FELT GOD'S PHYSICAL SUSTENANCE AS I HAVE SINCE KARA'S DEATH.

YOUR NOTE WAS MOST UNEXPECTED BUT CAME AT A TIME WHEN I REALLY NEEDED THE ENCOURAGEMENT. I NEEDED TO KNOW THAT I WAS NOT THE ONLY ONE WHO HAS LOST A SPOUSE AT SUCH A YOUNG AGE AND WAS LEFT TO CARE FOR A CHILD. THANK YOU!

I'M WONDERING IF YOU WOULD FEEL COMFORTABLE CONNECTING USING MORE MODERN TECHNOLOGY, I.E. SENDING AN EMAIL AND/OR GIVING YOU A CALL. (UNLIKE YOU, I AM NOT A VERY FLUID WRITER.) IF YOU DON'T, I UNDERSTAND. I KNOW IT WOULD HELP ME TO WORK THROUGH SOME STUFF. THANKS AGAIN AND GOD BLESS!

BRETT JOHNSON

P.S. MY PHONE NUMBER AND EMAIL ARE ON THE FLIP SIDE OF THIS.

P.P.S. AS I WAS WRITING THIS NOTE TO YOU, A TV NEWS SEGMENT CAME ON ABOUT A PROFESSIONAL ATHLETE WHO HAD GONE THROUGH SOME MAJOR AND SERIOUS HEALTH ISSUES. HE IS NOW RECOVERED AND MADE THE FOLLOWING STATEMENT: "LIFE DOESN'T HOLD ANY PROMISES, JUST PROMISE!"

She reread the letter a few times, thinking about his words. It was short, but very direct. It was clear that he had appreciated the note that she had sent to him. It was also clear that he was interested in corresponding again.

Am I interested in corresponding again? she wondered. She wasn't sure, but she did know that she had been excited to read the letter that she had just received from him, as evidenced by the fact that she read it before the other two in the stack. Her gut told her that she was interested, but the thought of talking to him personally on the phone made her feel nervous for reasons she couldn't quite understand.

She decided she would think on it for a little while. *I'll just give it a little time,* she told herself.

Before putting the letter away, she looked at his final note with the quote from the professional athlete. "Life doesn't hold any promises, just promise!" she read. She completely understood the first part. Life surely didn't hold any promises, or else Andy would never have died. She contemplated the second part. *Did this correspondence with Brett show promise?* The answer to that question lay in God's hands.

CHAPTER THIRTEEN

Brett

Brett usually went to his mailbox daily and checked his email multiple times a day, but he couldn't exactly say that he had been excited to do either task in the past. Now, with the anticipation of possibly receiving either another letter or an email from Gina, he checked his email twice as often and went directly to his mailbox as soon as he arrived home each night.

The first time he consciously realized that he was doing this was when he stubbed his toe on a step in his rush to get to the mailbox as quickly as possible. After the initial pain had subsided and he had taken a deep breath, he had chuckled at himself for his clumsiness and ridiculous boyish excitement about further correspondence with Gina. *Why do I care if I hear from her again?* he wondered. *She's written me one letter and I've written one back, and both of our letters were consoling each other about our losses. Heck, I've never even met her in person before!* He didn't really have an answer for himself. All he knew was that he liked hearing from her.

About a week later he checked his personal email during his lunch break at school, and there at the top of his inbox was an email with the name Oldham in it. His pulse quickened a bit as he immediately recognized it as Gina's and opened it.

Hey Brett,

Thank you for the response to my letter, especially considering that you had to track down my current address! I really can't believe that I accidentally wrote my old Mora address down as the return address. Maybe it's because I had to write "Mora" down for your address, and my brain just spit out my old address in the process. I seriously felt like smacking myself upside the head when I read that on your envelope! Sorry about that!

I am glad that my letter was able to offer you come encouragement. I lost Andy in the spring while you just lost your wife this fall, so I've had a few more months to heal and can firmly say that you will get through this. Especially since you have God on your side, you will make it through.

You said in your letter that you had never felt God's physical sustenance as you have since Kara's death. That has been exactly the way I have felt over the past six months. When I have to wake up in the middle of the night with Nathan (I am sure you can relate since you have a little one!), I pray and feel God encouraging my heart to keep persevering through the hard times. During Nathan's nap times, I have been making it a priority to read my Bible, and lately it has seemed like every story or section of scripture that I read has something that talks directly to me and my situation. It hasn't always been like that in the past, but since Andy died it's as if God is talking directly to me every time I read scripture. I have especially been enjoying the Psalms lately, since David is just so honest with God about his pain and his victories. It reminds me that other people have been through the highs and lows of life, and it reminds me that I am not alone in this battle. God is with me - and God is with you.

On a lighter note, I see in your email address that you have the word "sauna" in it. Do you like saunas or something? Do you own one? Just curious.

I personally have never been in one. I should try it sometime.

Thanks again for your encouraging note in response to mine. Like you said, for some reason it really makes a difference to know that there is someone else out there who has been through the exact same thing.

-Gina

Psalm 1: "Blessed is the man that walks not in the counsel of the wicked, nor stands in the way of sinners, nor sits in the seat of scoffers, but his delight is in the law of Jehovah, and on his law does he meditate day and night. And he shall be like a tree planted by the streams of water, that brings forth its fruit in its season, whose leaf also does not wither, and whatsoever he does shall prosper." I like the imagery in this passage. I like to picture myself as that tree planted by the stream of water that will eventually bring forth fruit again.

P.S. I like dorky jokes. I have one for you: What do you call a deer with no eyes? No eye deer.

Brett laughed out loud at the joke. It might have been a dorky joke, but it did the trick. It felt good to laugh.

He read through the email one more time quickly before the bell rang, signaling the end of his lunch and indicating that the students would be arriving soon. *How does lunch always go by so quickly?* Brett wondered for probably the hundredth time during his teaching career. Their lunches were a half an hour exactly from the end of one class to the passing time of the next class, but by the time he got things put away from one class and got things ready for the next class, it seemed like he only had about fifteen minutes to shovel down his lunch. *Ah, the life of a teacher,* he thought to himself. It was an awesome job, but sometimes having life regimented by the ring of a bell all day was a little stressful.

He made a mental note that he would have to type a response later that evening after Grant went to bed. That was his golden hour where he actually had a whole hour to himself, with no demands from students or his little baby. Brett time. And he knew exactly how he was going to use it.

* * * * * * * * * *

Later that night, after he had put Grant to bed, Brett sat down at his computer and read Gina's email once again and made a mental note of the things she talked about so he could include them in his reply. He then clicked on "compose" and typed away.

Gina,

Thank you for the email. I wasn't sure if you were going to feel comfortable corresponding with me any further, and I was happy to see that you did. Also, don't worry about the wrong return address thing. I actually found it funny, and it really wasn't that much work tracking it down. I actually got the address from Kara's mom, who grew up in the same church your parents now attend. It really is a small world.

To answer your question, I do love saunas! One of my friends introduced me to the positive effects of taking a sauna, and I got hooked the first time. This might sound strange, but there's something about sweating profusely that makes you feel like your body is purging itself of all the toxins inside and that your mind is purging itself of any worries at the same time. You should try it sometime. To be honest, I like saunas so much that I want to build one at my house someday. Then I can go as often as I wish!

I am going to take your advice about reading my Bible when Grant wakes up at night. I think I will even try reading the Psalms. I have read the Bible all the way through once, but it would be good to spend more time in one book, especially one where David talks openly about the highs and lows of life. Grant still wakes up at least once at night, so that would be a perfect way to spend that time. That might keep me from just sitting there and thinking about how much I miss Kara, which is what I usually do at night.

I look forward to hearing from you,

Brett

Proverbs 3:5-6 (one of my favorites): "Trust in The Lord with all your heart and lean not on your own understanding. In all your ways acknowledge Him, and He will make your paths straight."

P.S. I liked the joke. I actually laughed out loud. Keep them coming.

Brett read it through once, just to make sure he didn't have any embarrassing typos, and pressed "send." He let out a big sigh and ran his hand through his blond hair.

Tired out from the day, he headed to the bathroom to get ready for bed. He looked himself in the eye in the mirror and said aloud, "The ball is in your court on this one, Lord. I don't even know what to think about all of this."

After brushing his teeth, he went to his room, peeled back the covers, and climbed in. Just before shutting off the light, he looked over at his nightstand and saw a close-up picture of Kara holding Grant, and as he stared at it, his eyes started to tear up. He reached out and touched the picture, wistfully wishing he could see those blue eyes in real life just one more time.

He thought it was strange that he could have such contradictory emotions within the span of a few hours. One minute he had felt happy, even hopeful for his life and future, and the next he felt such pangs of loneliness that he wanted to pull the covers over his head and not wake up for a very long time.

After turning off the light, he whispered, "Goodnight, Kara. I miss you so much." A tear slipped down his cheek and onto the pillow as he closed his eyes and silently prayed for comfort and a good night's sleep.

Chapter Fourteen

Gina

Gina looked down at little Nathan playing on the living room floor. He had just learned to sit up and seemed very proud of himself, especially when he was able to stay upright after reaching for a toy. He would look at Gina with a huge smile that lit up his face as if to say, "Look at me, Mama! I'm a big boy!"

Gina couldn't help but notice the similarities between Nathan and Andy. They both had a reddish tint to their hair, were long and lean, and had similar positive dispositions. Though she loved that Nathan was her one physical daily reminder of Andy, it did make her miss him more intensely. Shortly after Andy's death, there were times where she would spontaneously burst into tears simply from looking at her son.

After a while, Nathan started rubbing his eyes and falling over, which were two clear signs that it was bedtime. Gina scooped him up in her arms, nuzzled into his tummy, which sent him into a cacophony of giggles, and whispered, "It's time for bed, little guy."

After reading to him, feeding him a bottle, and changing him, Gina lay little Nathan down in his crib. She paused for a moment, looking down at him one last time before leaving the room. She continually marveled at the miracle of life; there were so many things that had to come together to have a healthy baby, and she made it a goal to never forget how blessed she really was.

She let out a contented sigh and slowly slipped out of the room. She headed to the living room and considered her options. She could keep chipping away at the novel that she had started reading six months ago, but she would probably have to reread part of it to remember what was going on in the story. The last thing she remembered was the main character (what was her name?) getting invited to a party at her co-worker's house. It was a murder mystery, so she assumed that was where the initial murder would take place. She picked up the novel, but then set it down after deciding that reading required too much mental energy, which she lacked at the present moment.

Her eyes wandered over to the television. She could watch something, but she wouldn't even know what to watch. There were a few shows she liked, but she had no idea what time they were on. She hadn't had much time for television in the past six months.

She glanced over at her laptop and remembered that she had wanted to do a few things online. She had a few bills to pay, a few work emails to send, and then she had one other task she had been meaning to do but hadn't yet. She nestled into her couch, pulled her favorite fleece blanket over her lap, and reached for her computer.

After completing the first two things on her list, she considered if she really wanted to do the third or not. It might be slightly cyber-stalkerish if she did it, but her curiosity was killing her. She just had to see what Brett looked like. After she had written that first letter and then emailed Brett, her mind had wandered into the realm of imagining what he looked like, and she just couldn't stop thinking about it. She was annoyed at herself and wasn't exactly sure why it mattered, but she wanted to see a picture just the same. The only problem was that she wasn't sure where she could locate a picture of him. Then, a few days ago, in the middle of cooking dinner, it had occurred to her that she could look up Brett's picture on his school website. School websites always had pictures of their staff online. She had laughed at herself, since it always seemed like she got epiphanies doing the most mundane things like cooking or cleaning.

Anyway, she now found herself at that crossroad. She felt like if she looked him up, she was crossing over some mental threshold to the "next level." She sighed and ran her fingers through her brown curls that cascaded over the top of her head. *It might be better to just email back and forth a few more times,* she reasoned with herself. *But then again, I really want to see what he looks like,* she thought.

Her curiosity won out over her logic and she typed in the high school's name. The home page came up, and she searched the tabs and found the "staff" link. She clicked on that, which led her to a page of all the staff members. She found Brett's name and clicked on it, and that led to a separate page with his picture, the classes he taught, and a contact form.

She zeroed in on his picture. He had a full head of blond hair and piercingly blue eyes. He had a prominent brow with sandy-colored eyebrows. *Hmm,* she thought to herself. *I guess he's attractive, but it's hard to tell from a picture.* She felt a little disappointed in the fact that she didn't feel instantly and intensely attracted to him, but then quickly got annoyed at herself. *What did I expect, anyway?* she chided herself. *Did I think I would be totally blown away by him or something? Did I want to be totally blown away?*

She sighed and was just about to close the laptop when she remembered that she had only checked her work email, not her personal one. She looked at the time and paused for a moment, but decided it wouldn't hurt to check quickly before she went to bed.

After signing in, she saw an email from Brett at the top of her inbox. She took a deep breath and opened it up.

After reading it through, she realized that she was smiling. He had actually liked her dorky joke. Her friends always rolled their eyes at her when she recited a joke she had found on a candy wrapper or online. *Perhaps I've just had the wrong audience,* she thought to herself. *Time to get a new one...*

With that thought, she read Brett's email through one more time and then pressed "compose." Though she was tired, her mind found the words rather quickly as her fingers clicked on the keyboard.

Brett,

Thanks for your response. I am especially glad that you appreciate my jokes. Maybe you were just trying to be polite, but I will keep the jokes coming just the same. My friends just roll their eyes at me when I tell jokes, so you can be my new sounding board for them. Just to warn you, you may regret someday that you asked for more!

You may have convinced me to try a sauna sometime soon. I am not sure I will love it in the same way that you do (sweating profusely doesn't sound that fun to me), but I will at least give it a try. I'll let you know how it goes!

I am also happy to hear that you are going to try reading the Psalms at night when little Grant wakes up. I just know that you will be encouraged by the raw sincerity of David's words. Whether he is happy, angry, or worried, he just puts it out there to God. It inspires me to do the same.

I'll tell you a few other things about me that might give you a better picture of what I'm like. I am a physical therapist, so I work at a clinic where I help to rehabilitate people after surgeries and accidents. To be honest, most of my patients are older people who have undergone hip surgery or something similar, but I do get some younger ones. My favorites are the athletes who are trying to make it back on the field. They always have extra motivation to get better and they actually do the exercises I assign them to do at home, unlike the majority of my older patients. Also, I am pretty outgoing and love to hang out with family and friends. I have always felt that, besides God, people are the one true joy in life and you have to treasure them. Andy's death has made that even more apparent to me.
Now that you've told me about you, what is the rest of your family like? How about baby Grant? Maybe tell me a little about them in the next email.

Gina

Philippians 4:12-13 - "...in everything and in all things I have learned the secret both to be filled and to be hungry, both to abound and to be in want. I can do ALL things through Christ who strengthens me." I love that one. It makes me feel like God can help me through anything (and he has).

P.S. Now that I know you specifically teach math, here is a dorky math joke for you (feel free to use it in class!): Why was six afraid of seven? Because seven "eight" nine. Ha!

Gina read it over a few times and pressed "send." Then she checked the time and made a mental note that she was going to be really tired the next day.

After getting ready for bed, she felt like her body melted into her pillow and bedding. Before falling asleep, she whispered, "God, if possible, please help Nathan sleep in a little tomorrow. I think this Mama needs it."

CHAPTER FIFTEEN

Brett

Over the past month, Brett and Gina had emailed back and forth multiple times a week. He found himself looking forward to hearing from her more and more, which both excited him and bothered him at the same time.

He wasn't sure what to think of the whole thing. He knew, logically speaking, that he and Gina were just friends. She was someone who was going through the same thing at the same time, so it was natural that the two of them would relate to each other so well.

However, though his head told him that all of those things were true, in his heart of hearts, he knew that Gina had become something more than just a friend to him. What exactly she had become, he wasn't sure, but he did know that he had grown to care about her in some capacity. There was something forming between the two of them that he didn't know how to define or even put into words. And he hadn't even met her yet in person.

He still missed Kara immensely, though the raw pain that he had felt immediately following her death had lessened into kind of a dull ache. Almost everything he saw reminded him of her in some way, whether it was something obvious like a picture from the house or something subtle like a maple leaf outside. There were so many memories. Everywhere.

Though he missed Kara more than he could express, he was surprised at how well he was functioning on a day-to-day basis. When he had been in the hospital with Kara before she died and she was on life support, the mere thought of living life without her had seemed so daunting and crushing, as if the very air he breathed was being sucked out of his lungs and he would be left limp and lifeless, a shell of a reminder of who he once was. Immediately following her death,

Grant had kept him going, though it felt like he was functioning on autopilot for many of those days. Then, with time, he slowly started to heal, until one day he realized that he was actually enjoying parts of life again. Life could and would go on, even without Kara beside him on earth. There was still beauty all around him; he just had to open his eyes to see it. His family, friends, and time spent reading the Bible had reassured him of that truth.

Now he found himself at somewhat of a fork in the road. Down one path, he could see far ahead, picturing himself living as he had been, slowly learning to live life again, emailing Gina once in a while as friends. Down another road, which was not as clear due to having a bend in it and dense vegetation blocking the view, he saw himself picking up the phone and calling Gina, moving into another realm in the woods, one that could be tangled and jumbled and full of the unknown.

He sighed and sat down on his living room couch. He hated forks in the road. He was a man who always liked to know the plan, playing it safe in his mathematical world where all could be figured out in some sort of equation. As he sat there, his eyes wandered over to a framed poem on the wall. How ironic. It was "The Road Not Taken" by Robert Frost, one of Kara's favorites. He read it through, noting that there couldn't be a better poem to define his thoughts at the moment.

The Road Not Taken

Two roads diverged in a yellow wood,
And sorry I could not travel both
And be one traveler, long I stood
And looked down one as far as I could
To where it bent in the undergrowth;

Then took the other, as just as fair,
And having perhaps the better claim,
Because it was grassy and wanted wear;
Though as for that the passing there
Had worn them really about the same,

And both that morning equally lay
In leaves no step had trodden black.
Oh, I kept the first for another day!
Yet knowing how way leads on to way,
I doubted if I should ever come back.

I shall be telling this with a sigh
Somewhere ages and ages hence:
Two roads diverged in a wood, and I—
I took the one less traveled by,
And that has made all the difference.

He felt like that traveler. The lines, "Yet knowing how way leads on to way/I doubted if I should ever come back," especially stuck out to him. If he took that first step on the other path and called Gina, there was no way he could come back to the first path of safety and security of what was known. That just wasn't how life worked.

The comfort of the first path tempted him, but the potential of the second path intrigued him. Though the terrain was perhaps dense and rough ahead, the thrill of adventure awaited him.

He stood up. He was sick of always playing it safe in life. And with that, he took his first step on the path into the unknown.

* * * * * * * * * *

Over three hours later, Brett put the phone down. The adventure had begun.

CHAPTER SIXTEEN

Gina

As Gina lay in bed, she knew she was going to have a hard time falling asleep that night. *Three hours?* She couldn't remember the last time she had talked to someone for three hours on the phone. The last time was probably when she and Andy had started dating.

Hmm. Andy. Gina wondered what he would think of all of this. She thought back to his final weeks when he was in hospice and they had conversed about the future. Andy had told her that he wanted her to be happy and marry again if he died. He had said it and meant it. Though she knew that and believed it, there was still a part of her that felt conflicted about moving ahead with Brett.

But he had called. She couldn't help that. Again, she felt like she had crossed a bridge into another realm of their relationship, whatever that was at the present moment, and there was no going back.

They had talked about many things, but the majority of their conversation had centered around surviving the death of a spouse, specifically how each of them was handling grief; how to handle a six-month old boy; and how to keep oneself together in the midst of it all.

Another topic they had hit on was how they both had in-laws who were struggling with loss, namely Andy's dad and Kara's parents. That was difficult for everyone involved.

The last part of the conversation had touched on how amazing it was that the two of them had found each other and had been able to form a friendship that had really helped the two of them to grieve. They both felt that God was using each of them to help in the healing process of the other.

Gina couldn't believe how easy it was to talk to Brett. She honestly couldn't recall one awkward moment in the entire conversation. One topic segued into another, and before she knew it, three hours had passed. *Three hours*. She still couldn't believe it.

Even though she was further along in the grieving process than Brett due to the fact that Andy had died in April and Brett's wife had died in October, it had felt so good to actually *hear* someone's voice who could relate with her inmost thoughts about the raw pain incurred from losing a spouse. When he spoke about what he had gone through and how he was feeling, Gina felt like he was talking about her. She had felt those very things: loss, pain, frustration, and emptiness. But she had also felt the other things he spoke of: love, hope, and a greater dependence on one's faith in God.

Her mind was spinning. There was no way she was going to be able to sleep for a while. She got out of bed, went into the living room, and grabbed the mystery novel that she hadn't opened for a while. Reading always helped relax her mind and eventually her body. She made it to Chapter Four and then drifted off somewhere shortly after the detective arrived to investigate...

* * * * * * * * *

Gina woke up to the sound of Nathan crying in the morning. She opened her eyes groggily and yawned so long her eyes watered. She slowly looked over at the clock.

Her eyes widened and she sat up quickly. It was 7:00 already? Usually she woke up by 6:00, even without an alarm. She must have forgotten to set it last night.

She was going to have to get a move on if she wanted to make it to work on time. She had to feed Nathan, get him dressed, get herself ready, drop him off at daycare, and make it to work by 8:30. That was no small feat with a little one.

Despite being a little rushed, Gina found herself humming as she got herself and Nathan ready. She kept remembering bits and pieces of her conversation with Brett the prior night and it turned a hectic morning into a pleasant one.

She found herself a little absent-minded at work that day. One of her midday patients had to ask her a question three times before it registered. He had been a little annoyed at her, so she made it a goal to keep more focused on her work the rest of the day. *Seriously, Gina,* she chided. *It was just a phone call. Focus.*

She made it through the rest of the day without any of her patients needing to repeat questions, and after picking Nathan up, making dinner for the two of them, and putting him to bed, she checked her email, and there was one from Brett at the top of her inbox. She smiled and opened it right away.

Hey Gina,

I wanted to share a few thoughts regarding our conversation last night. I feel like I have to get some of my thoughts and emotions out, even if I'm repeating myself. Please forgive me if I do.

First, I am hoping we can pray together in some of our future conversations. I want us to seek God's wisdom (both individually and communally) through this friendship-building process. I hope that next time we talk, you would feel comfortable with this.

Second, I don't know if I made this crystal clear, but you need to know that what's truly most important to me is that both of us are following God's will. If He means for us to be just a "grief and loss support group" and that's it, so be it. However, if God's plan is more than that, then I am game.

Regarding His will: I feel I've been following God's will through this whole ordeal, yet I can't believe where I'm at in this grieving process. Very few things have come about as I would have expected them to. This is why a huge part of me is struggling right now. I figured I would be paralyzed by grief for months, yet I'm not. I figured that every time I saw a picture and remembered a memory, I'd have to sit and cry it out. I don't do that. I still cry at times, but not as often as I thought I would. Christian music, a supportive network of friends and family, and most importantly God's Word has helped me focus solely on Jesus and not on the pain and loss. Grief really is completely unique to the individual.

Along the same lines, I am very thankful that God has brought you into my life. Your friendship has been instrumental in helping me get through this difficult time. I just wanted you to know that I appreciate you, and I am excited to get to know you better in the future, whatever the future may entail.

I just wanted you to know a few of my thoughts. Hope to talk to you soon,

Brett

1 Corinthians 15:58 - "Therefore, my dear brothers, stand firm. Let nothing move you. Always give yourselves fully to the work of The Lord, because you know that your labor in The Lord is not in vain."

Gina smiled again and leaned back on the couch. She really did like hearing from Brett. She wasn't sure where it all was going, but she did know that she was going to write him back.

CHAPTER SEVENTEEN

Brett

Brett found himself smiling the next few days, and he wasn't normally a smiley kind of person. Usually he was a little more straight-faced and serious, fitting his logical type-A personality. But he just couldn't help himself.

It had been a difficult decision to pick up the phone and take that next step of calling Gina, but he had no regrets. Hearing her voice for the first time had made all the difference. For some reason, when he actually heard her say her thoughts aloud versus sending them over email, they seemed so much more meaningful and insightful.

He still couldn't believe that they had talked for three hours straight. He wasn't sure if he had ever talked to someone for three hours straight before. He usually was more of a listener who kept his thoughts to himself, but he had turned into quite the chatterbox once he had gotten on the phone with Gina. He wasn't quite sure what had come over him. She was definitely easy to talk to, which he thought was an important quality. He could sense her positive personality beaming through over the phone, and it was contagious.

Though he truly did feel like God had brought Gina across his path, he didn't know in what capacity she was meant to be in his life. Right now, they were just friends, but Brett felt the pull to be open to something more in the future.

Because he didn't totally feel confident in his emotional state at the present moment, given the fact that Kara had died only a few months ago and he was incredibly lonely, he decided he was going to enlist the help of a few of his friends. He had a close group of guy friends who had kept him afloat during Kara's death and shortly after, and he knew he could depend on them for anything. If he told them about Gina and asked them to pray for him and give him good counsel, they would do it, no questions asked. Brett knew that his friends would keep him accountable to making wise decisions, and that was what he needed.

After Grant had gone to sleep for the evening, Brett emailed three of his friends and threw out a few dates to get together so he could talk to them. He wanted to explain this one face-to-face.

Right after he pressed "send," he was about to close out of his email when he heard the new mail ding and saw he had a new message from Gina. He didn't waste any time in opening it.

Brett,

Here are a few of my thoughts on your thoughts and on our phone conversation the other night (hope that made sense).

First of all, I have no problem praying any time. Prayer is great. I think that is the key to keep God in the center of anything and everything.

Also, I don't think that it's a bad or embarrassing or heartless thing to not be completely "crushed" by the loss of a spouse. Sure, it is difficult and you really feel like a piece of you is missing, because it is. But as a Christian, your outlook on death is very different than others. We look at death as a reward. What better place to be than in the arms of Jesus. It's not like either of us surrendered our spouse to something awful beyond this life. We let them go into a place that is so incredible that the Bible only touches on how great it is. How can we not be happy for Andy and Kara? They are so incredibly happy and peaceful right now. They are home; we are not. I've said many times that I'm happy for Andy, but I'm sad for me, because it stinks to be left behind. So I wouldn't feel bad about not feeling crushed, because as much as we tried to make our spouses happy and make this life great for them, Jesus will only do better in heaven (home). I think that those who don't have Jesus or believe in heaven are more paralyzed by grief because they don't understand what joy there is in death. Andy's memorial service was a going-home party. I even had pizza, pop, jello, and chocolate chip cookies served at the service. These were Andy's favorite and I wanted a party for him! Also, I think that the incredible prayer support that we have received from others has helped tremendously in keeping us afloat.

In thinking about how our parents (meaning Andy's and Kara's parents) respond to grief and loss of a son or daughter, I think that perhaps the loss is harder for them because they lost a son or daughter. There is no getting that type of relationship back. Andy was an only son, so that has hit his dad really hard. (Was Kara an only daughter?) Conversely, we as spouses may at sometime (Lord willing) have the opportunity to have a marriage-type relationship again. Of course we will NEVER be able to replace Andy or Kara. No one will ever hold your hand, give you a hug, or tease you just the way that your spouse did. But it is possible to have another spouse, unlike our in-laws where there is never the opportunity to have another son or daughter like that again.

Andy said something several weeks before he even went to the hospital for the last time (we didn't know he was terminal yet). We talked about the possibility that he might not make it through this cancer stuff. It was one of the very few conversations we had about this, and it was very short! Drew said, "Time will heal, but there will always be a scar." I really believe that now. Time is healing me, but there will always be the hurt and pain that my best friend is no longer around. Time and processing the loss does cut the stinging feeling of the loss, but there will never cease to be some hard times. And it's okay when they do come, and it's okay if they don't come often. God is amazing in the way the He heals. I really think that it's okay to look forward to the future and to get excited about what else this life might hold. I think that even in dealing with grief, part of it entails looking ahead and getting excited. When you said you have emotions coming from both ends of the spectrum, that is normal, and you would go crazy if you had emotions from only one end of the spectrum. You would either have terrible grief and be stuck in a pit, or you would be on cloud nine and be really annoying to everyone around!

Also, all of our phone conversations don't need to be totally deep and intellectual. I wouldn't mind just goofing off at times. I don't want to get sucked into too much seriousness! Perhaps I will have to lighten the mood with another joke.

Norwegian joke:
Lars: Ole, stand in front of my car and tell me if my turn signals are working.
Ole: Yes, no, yes, no, yes, no…

Here is a dumb joke my dad told me:
Why do gorillas have big nostrils?
Because they have big fingers.

Call any time.

Gina

Brett smiled at the jokes. He especially liked the Norwegian one.

He reread the email and found a few things she said to be exceptionally insightful. For one, he appreciated Gina's words about their spouses being and heaven and how that helps the ones left behind not to be so sad. The more he thought about it, that was one of the reasons he wasn't completely devastated by Kara's death; he knew she was peaceful and happy in heaven. Also, what Gina said about Kara's and Andy's parents completely made sense to him. They didn't have the hope of another son or daughter, but Gina and Brett both had the hope for someone else in the future. Lastly, he thought her final comments about him being so serious, and he knew it was true. He needed to lighten up. He liked that she felt comfortable enough with him to say it.

Brett looked up and whispered, "God, where is this going? What do you want to happen with all of this?" He sat quietly for a few minutes and felt a sense of peace come over him. He still wasn't sure what was going to happen, but he felt like God had everything under control, and that was enough.

CHAPTER EIGHTEEN

Gina

Another month had passed and Christmas was fast approaching. Gina felt an extra spring in her step and an extra dose of joy during this Christmas season. She and Brett had been talking multiple times a week on the phone, with most of the phone calls lasting two or three hours. They had also continued to email, as well. She still wasn't sure what to make of it all, but she did know that Brett had become one of her best friends in a short amount of time and that he made her feel happy when she spoke with him.

Gina found herself smiling for no reason in particular as she played with little Nathan on the floor. She couldn't believe how big he was getting and how much he was changing. It was amazing to her how a baby could be born frail and helpless, and in just seven months could be sitting up, looking around, smiling, laughing, and eating some solid foods. *I wish I could learn things at such a rapid pace now,* Gina thought to herself.

Gina heard a knock on the door and looked at Nathan with a smile. She said, "Grandma and Grandpa are here. Let's go to the door and see them!" She scooped Nathan up from the floor and went to the door.

Her mom was peeking through the window on the door and waving at Nathan. His face erupted into a smile and he giggled. Gina opened the door and gave her mom a hug. She looked behind her mom and saw her dad involved in a struggle with a Christmas tree. He was attempting to get a good hold on it, but it kept slipping out of his grasp. He was definitely losing the battle.

"How's it going back there, Dad?" Gina teased.

He finally got a good grasp on the trunk, heaved it up in the air, and said, "I'll let you know in a minute. Clear the path, ladies!"

Gina and her mom moved out of the way and her dad crashed through the open door, losing a few needles on the way. He walked into the living room and said, "Where do you want this?"

"To the right of the couch by the window right there," Gina quickly answered, hoping her dad didn't hurt himself or knock anything over in the process.

He walked a few more steps and then plopped the tree over by the window. He stood up, put his hands behind his head, and took a few deep breaths. "I probably should have asked you where to put it before I picked it up!"

Gina laughed and walked up to her dad for a hug. He enfolded her in a big bear hug and said, "How's my girl and my favorite grandson?"

Gina rolled her eyes and said, "He's your only grandson, Dad. And to answer your question, we're holding our own." She looked at Nathan, still in her arms, and said, "Aren't we, Nathan? We're doing all right."

Her mom chimed in. "Your father and I bought you a Christmas tree because you mentioned you didn't have one up yet, and that's just preposterous. I didn't want to have to start calling you Ebenezer Scrooge."

Gina tilted her head and looked at her mom. "I was going to get around to it. I've been...busy."

Her mom put her hands out for Nathan and he raised his hands towards her. "Come here, sweetie." She kissed him on the cheek and said, "Have you been keeping your mom busy? Too busy to decorate for Christmas?"

Gina gave her mom an exasperated look. "Mom, I have decorated for Christmas...partially." She looked around the room and pointed out a few of her Christmas decorations. "I just haven't gotten to the tree part yet. You know that I prefer a real tree, but it's hard to get one strapped to my car and to haul it all by myself." She paused and giggled. "I mean, look at Dad. Hauling the tree here almost killed him, and he's a big, tough guy."

He pretended to look hurt. "I don't know what you're talking about. I totally dominated that tree."

Her mom nuzzled her face into Nathan's stomach and made him giggle. "Well, anyhow, we brought you a tree, so let's get some Christmas music on and decorate!"

Gina turned on her CD player, already loaded with Christmas CD's, and heard "The First Noel" begin to play. She then walked to her hallway closet and pulled out a box of Christmas tree decorations. She hauled it into the living room, sat on the couch, opened the box, and started pulling smaller containers out.

The top container housed her very favorite Christmas tree ornaments from childhood. She pulled out an angel one and said, "Remember this one, Mom?"

Her mom reached over and gently took it from Gina. "Oh, yes. I bought this for you when you were eight and then told you that you were my little angel." She looked up at Gina and added, "And you still are."

Gina smiled. "Oh, Mom. You are so cheesy sometimes."

Her dad put his hand on his wife's back. "And that's why we love her."

After putting her childhood decorations up, she pulled another container out of the big box. She hesitated for a moment, realizing that this container held ornaments that she and Andy had given each other over the years.

She reluctantly opened it and pulled out the first one. It was a Minnesota moose with clothespin antlers. She sighed and held it in her hand. Andy had given this to her because she had always wanted to see a moose in real life and never had seen one, so he had told her she could have a "moose sighting" every year around Christmas. Just remembering that moment when he gave it to her made her miss him so intensely that she felt like crying. Maybe this was secretly the reason she hadn't gotten a tree yet. So many memories were packed in that decoration box.

Her mom and dad noticed her mood change immediately. Her mom sat down on the couch next to her and said, "Are you okay, honey?"

She let her mom hug her and said, "Yeah, I just really miss him. This is my first Christmas without him, and it's hard sometimes."

It was quiet for a moment and then her dad, trying to lighten the mood, said, "Well, you still have us, baby girl. We're not going anywhere."

Gina smiled. "I know, Dad. Thanks."

Her mom must have thought it best to change the subject and said, "So, have you talked to what's-his-name lately?"

Gina rolled her eyes again. "You mean Brett?"

Her mom snapped her fingers. "Yeah, Brett." Her mom winked at her. "I was just teasing. I know his name. I mean, you talk about him enough. Anyway, have you talked to Brett lately?"

"Yes. We talked for two hours again last night."

Her mom's eyes widened. "Two hours. Wow." She put her hand on her hip. "What can you possibly have to say that lasts two hours?" Gesturing at the Christmas tree, she added, "No wonder you haven't had time to get a tree and decorate it."

Gina gave her mom a look. "I'm going to take the high road and ignore that comment, Mom." She paused and took a deep breath. "Anyway, we talk about lots of things. You know, life, death, babies, exasperating family members..." She gave her mom another look and smiled.

Her mom stuck her chin in the air. "I'm going to assume you mean other family members when you say that."

Her dad chimed in. "I just think it's so amazing that God allowed you to meet a friend who is going through exactly the same thing as you are. And, to top it off, he has a son almost the exact same age as Nathan. It's really quite incredible. No wonder you two have a lot to talk about."

Gina smiled. "Yeah. Plus, he's really easy to talk to. He's really become a good friend in the past few months."

Her mom's eyebrows arched. "Friend? Is that all he is? You two email back and forth multiple times a week and have two to three hour phone calls. I don't talk that much to my friends."

Gina let out an exasperated sigh. "Yes, Mom. Friend. I mean, I haven't even met him in person yet. How can he be more than a friend?"

"Yet?" Her mom looked at her curiously. "What do you mean by yet? Have you two planned to meet sometime soon?"

Gina shrugged her shoulders. "Well, we talked about maybe meeting after Christmas. You see, I get this free formula from work, and it has been upsetting Nathan's stomach, but it's the exact same kind he uses for Grant. I was going to give it to him since I've switched to a different brand and don't use it anyway."

Her mom gave her a knowing smile. "Hmm. So you're only meeting to exchange formula? He's just going to come to the door, get the formula, and leave?"

Gina's face turned red and she looked away sheepishly. "Well, I'm sure we might hang out for a while. I mean, it is a long drive for him and everything. He might stay for dinner or something."

Her dad clapped her on the back. "Well, I think meeting him is a great idea. Like I said, you two have a lot in common. Besides, it's always more fun to talk to someone in person."

Her mom gave her a hug. "I think it's a great idea, too, honey. I was just teasing you before. She leaned out from Gina and looked her in the eye. "Your father and I have been praying for you. And for Brett, too."

Gina smiled. "You mean what's-his-name?" Her eyes twinkled.

Her mom flashed her a smile back. "Yes. What's-his-name. Exactly."

She squeezed her mom's hand. "I know you have been, Mom. And thank you."

* * * * * * * * * *

Three weeks later, shortly after the holidays, Gina found herself nervously awaiting Brett's arrival.

He's just coming to get the formula, she told herself. *Then why am I so nervous?* she wondered.

She straightened the couch pillows for the umpteenth time. Nathan was taking a nap and was due to wake up soon, and she wasn't sure what to do with herself until Brett arrived.

She didn't have to wonder very long because she heard a knock at the door. She stood up, straightened her shirt, and walked to the doorway.

When she opened up the door, she was pleasantly surprised. He was much better-looking in person than the picture on the school website. His blue eyes especially stood out to her as he smiled at her.

Gina cleared her throat. "Hey." She realized she was just staring and added, "I mean, welcome. Come on in." She gestured into her living room.

As Brett walked through the doorway, she felt like another door was opening, one that would take their relationship to a whole other level. And she was ready for it.

CHAPTER NINETEEN

Brett

His heart had been pounding as he had approached her door. When the door opened and he saw her for the first time, he had only one thought: *Beautiful.*

She was tall and very athletic-looking. Her natural brown curls edged her face and accentuated her brown eyes. When she flashed him a smile, it lit up her face in a way that showed off her natural beauty.

After she gestured for him to walk inside, he cleared his throat and found his voice. "Well, I made it. It wasn't too hard to find."

Gina gave him another smile as he sat down on the living room couch. "I told you it was easy to find. And here you are." She sat down on one of the easy chairs.

"And here I am." He looked around him. "It's nice and cozy in here." He nodded towards the fireplace. "I love fireplaces. They always make it seem warmer in the winter time."

"Yeah. It's one of my favorite features of the house. I really lucked out."

He noticed the Christmas tree and decorations. "I see it's still Christmas around here," he teased her.

She gave him a sheepish smile. "Yeah. I didn't get the tree up until recently. My mom and dad actually bought it for me and helped put it up. I thought the least I could do was leave it up for a while."

He nodded. "Right. I mean, it would be disrespectful to take it down right away after they did all of that work," he said teasingly.

"Exactly. That, and I just love Christmas. I always feel sad when I have to take the tree down. Then Christmas is officially over."

"Yeah. I always dread the end of Christmas break. For one, Christmas is my favorite holiday and I never want it to be over.

Besides that, I know I have to go back to work and grade stacks of math assignments when Christmas is over. Which happens to be this coming Monday for me." He grimaced at the thought of going back to work.

Gina laughed. "At least you get a Christmas break. I just had a few days off around Christmas and a few for New Year's. I could go for a few more."

He smiled. "I suppose no matter how much vacation time I had I would always want more. It's probably human nature to want to loaf around forever. But kids need to learn. So I guess I have to go back."

"And people need their physical therapy." She let out a sigh. "But I had a great Christmas. Nathan sure loved seeing his grandparents." Her face lit up in a big smile. "And he sure loved getting presents. Although he was more interested in the wrapping paper and boxes than the actual present."

He couldn't help but laugh. "Yeah, Grant, too. He just sat on the floor ripping up wrapping paper for a while with a huge smile on his face. We should have just gotten him wrapping paper for Christmas. It would have been a lot less expensive."

"So you went to both sides of grandparents, too, right?" Gina asked.

Brett's eyebrows knit together, thinking. "Yeah. We went to both sides." He paused. "It went okay."

Gina raised her eyebrows. "Just okay? What do you mean?"

He hesitated, weighing his words. "Well, my side of the family was just like normal. We ate, talked, and played games. The norm for the Johnson's. But Kara's side...well, it was a little awkward."

"Awkward how?"

He cleared his throat. "As I've shared with you before, Kara's parents are having an extremely difficult time letting her go. It was very obvious that they haven't come as far in the grieving process as I have." He sighed. "Instead of it being a happy celebration of Christ's birth, it seemed to be a sad remembrance of Kara. It was just hard."

Gina gave him a sympathetic look. "I'm sorry to hear that. That's tough. I was kind of wondering how that would go."

Brett ran his hand through his blond hair. "Yeah. Not so great. To top it off, I told them about you and how we've become good friends. I explained how you have pretty much gone through the exact same situation as I have and how God has been using both of us to help each other heal."

"And?" Gina questioned.

"And...it was a total fail. I think the only thing they took out of it was that I had met someone else. It was kind of quiet the rest of the time we were there. I don't know how to make them understand." He paused and looked out the window. "I don't know if they are ready to try to understand."

Gina put her hand on top of his, which was resting on the arm of the couch. "Just give it time. And a lot of prayer." She looked right into his eyes. "I'll pray, too."

"Thanks," Brett said, and meant it. He would take all the prayer he could get.

A beeper went off in the kitchen somewhere. Gina cleared her throat and said, "Dinner's done." She looked at her watch. "I can't believe Nathan is still sleeping. How about you and I eat and then I'll get him up. Then we can actually talk."

Though Brett was sorry that the beeper had taken Gina's hand away from the top of his, he was ready to eat. He hadn't eaten very much for lunch. "Sounds good to me. I know how that is. That's why I left Grant home with my mom and dad, who are visiting for a few days." He smelled the scent wafting over to him as Gina opened the oven. "What's for dinner? It smells delicious!"

Gina pulled a big roasting pan out of the oven. "Baked chicken, potatoes, and carrots. I figured I couldn't go wrong with chicken!"

Brett smiled. "It's true. And it happens to be one of my favorites. Good call."

As he helped Gina set the table for two, Brett couldn't help but feel like whatever this was with Gina was blossoming into something bigger than he had ever expected. And for some reason, the thought didn't scare him at all.

CHAPTER TWENTY

Gina

"So, how did it go?" her mom asked on the other end of the line.

Gina smiled. "Great, Mom. In fact, it went so well that Brett almost forgot the formula when he was leaving! And that was the whole point of him coming in the first place!"

"Mm-hmm. So you've told me. But I didn't buy that the first time you told me and I still don't. There's a lot more to this than friends exchanging formula, missy," her mom teased.

Gina feigned shock on the other end of the line. "Mother! What am I going to do with you?"

"Oh, you love me and you know it. Anyway, you do have to admit there was more to it than just the exchange of formula," her mom pressed.

Gina threw up her hands in the air. "Okay, okay, Mom. I admit. There was more to it than just giving him the formula." She could picture her mom smiling smugly on the other end of the line.

"Exactly. Anyway, I need some specifics. I mean, this is the first time you've met him in person. What did you think? Did you find him attractive? How was dinner? What did you two talk about?"

"Whoa, whoa, whoa, Mom. One question at a time," Gina said, feeling like a machine gun of questions had been unleashed on her.

"Okay, first things first," her mom replied. "Did you find him attractive?"

Gina smiled and twisted a curl around her finger. "Actually, yeah, I did. He was much cuter than the picture online on his school web site that I looked up a while ago." She knew that would get her mom going.

"What? You looked him up online? You never told me that. You little cyber-stalker, you," she teased.

"I know, I know. But I was just so curious and had to see what he looked like. But his picture online definitely didn't do him any justice. He was way better-looking in person."

"How so?" her mom prodded.

"Well, his eyes really stood out to me. They were piercingly blue. And his hair was really blond and clean-cut. He must have just recently gotten a haircut. He had a pretty athletic build, too." She smiled just thinking about him. "He was just really handsome."

"Hmm," her mom said dreamily on the other end of the line. "Well, I'm glad you were attracted to him. No matter what people say to the contrary, there has to be some element of physical attraction there. Good. Now onto the next question. What did you serve for dinner?"

"You would have been proud of me, Mom. I made a chicken roast with potatoes and carrots." She could sense her mom beaming on the other end of the line.

"That's my girl," her mom said with a hint of pride in her voice. "So some of my cooking lessons growing up have paid off. And men do love a good roast. Very impressive, honey." She paused momentarily before unloading another question on Gina. "And what did you two talk about?"

Gina's eyebrows knotted up in concentration, trying to recall exactly what they had talked about. "Well, everything, Mom. It's kind of hard to pinpoint a few things. We just talked about...everything."

"Everything? Well, think harder. That's not specific enough for me," her mom challenged.

Gina twisted another curl around her finger, thinking. "Well, we talked a lot about the holidays and how they went for each of us."

"What did he have to say about that?" her mom asked.

"Well, he said that going to Kara's parents' house was kind of hard. They are still really...struggling with Kara's death. If you could remember, Mom, pray for them. It just sounds like a really hard situation overall."

"I will, honey," her mom assured her. "I can't imagine how difficult it would be to lose you, so I'm sure it's been so hard for them."

"It has." She sighed. "Anyway, we talked a lot about the boys and what they have been doing lately. It's so funny to me that they are almost exactly the same age."

"That is a funny coincidence." Her mom paused on the other end, as if thinking. Then she added, "Or maybe it's not such a coincidence. Somehow I think that God worked all of this out to make something good out of something tragic. Only He could do that."

"Umm-hmm," Gina agreed after contemplating her mom's words.

"So, are you going to see him again? It sounds like you should after it went so well the first time."

Gina could picture her mom holding her breath on the other side of the line, awaiting her answer. "Actually, yes. And pretty soon. We planned a day to go skiing next weekend, since we discovered we both like to ski. Oh, and we are going to meet at a restaurant in Moose Lake, which is kind of in the middle of Mora and Duluth, to eat in the next few weeks."

"So, kind of an official date on the second one?" her mom prodded.

"Well, I don't know if I would call it a date. We're just meeting."

"Hmm," her mom said skeptically. "Is that what you call it when two people who are obviously interested in each other meet? A meeting? I call that a date. Maybe I'm way off base."

Gina sighed in exasperation. "Oh, call it what you want. We haven't really talked about dating or what our relationship status is at this point. We are just good friends who may or may not have a romantic inclination towards each other meeting on purpose. That's all."

Her mom snorted. "That sounds like a bunch of mumbo-jumbo to me. Anyway, do you know at which restaurant you'll be meeting? What do you think you'll wear? Do you need me to watch Nathan?"

Gina laughed. "Whoa, whoa, Mom, slow down. Yes, I think I might need you to watch Nathan. And have you been to Moose Lake? It's super tiny. I guess they only have a few restaurants, so it might be something like Subway or Dairy Queen. And I have no idea what I'll wear, Mom. I haven't even thought about it yet."

"Well, you want to look sharp, no matter where you're going. Maybe I'll help you pick something out when I come to watch Nathan. That would be fun!" her mom said excitedly.

"Oh, Mom. You do get excited about this stuff. Sure, you can help me pick something out. But it should be fun no matter what I wear."

"I know, sweetie. But you may as well look cute doing whatever it is you two decide to do!" her mom said.

* * * * * * * * * *

A few weeks later, Gina's mom arrived to watch Nathan, bustling in the doorway and announcing, "Grandma's here! Where's my little Nathan?"

Gina looked down at Nathan, who was playing with his blocks on the living room floor, and saw him smile in her mom's direction. He knew that voice.

"Hi, Mom. Come on in," she teased, noting the fact that her mom let herself in.

Her mom scooped up Nathan from the floor. "Hey, little man. Grandma's here to watch you so that your mom can go out on her date!"

Gina rolled her eyes. "Mom. It's not a date! We talked about this."

Her mom smiled. "Oh. Right." She started talking to Nathan again. "What I meant was that Grandma's here to watch you so that your mom can go on her outing that is really a date in disguise."

Gina put her hands on her hips. "Mo-om. Seriously. You are ridiculous."

Her mom shrugged her shoulders. "But you love me. And you're happy I'm here. Admit it."

Gina giggled. "Yes, Mom, I do love you and I am glad you are here. But you are still ridiculous."

Her mom started walking towards Gina's room. "Did you pick out something to wear yet? If so, I want to see it."

Gina trailed her mom into her bedroom. "By that you mean you want to approve it."

Her mom turned around and flashed her a smile. "Same thing." She spotted the three outfits Gina had laid out on the bed. She gestured towards them. "I take it that these three are your options?"

"Yep. I guess I don't really care what I wear, but I knew you wanted to help pick out my outfit, so I put a few out for you. Tell me what you think."

"Oh, you know I will." She looked at the first one on the left. "I like the red, but it might be too wild for a first date."

Gina cleared her throat and gave her mom a reproachful look.

Her mom got the hint and said, "Oh, sorry. I meant first outing." She moved on to the second outfit. "Hmm. I like this green shirt on you." She held it up to Gina. "It's definitely a good option." She then saw the third outfit. "Ooh, is this new? I like the yellow. It looks good against your brown curls. Definitely the yellow."

Gina smiled. She knew her mom would pick that one. "Sounds good, Mom. And yes, it is new. I actually bought something new for myself."

"Good for you, honey. I'll take Nathan out to the living room so you can change and finish getting ready."

"Thanks, Mom. You are the best!"

"And don't you forget it!" her mom said as she closed Gina's bedroom door.

About ten minutes later, Gina gave herself one last look in the mirror and waltzed out the door. She gave her mom and Nathan a kiss on the cheek and said, "I'm off! You know where everything is, Mom, so you should be fine. Remember he goes to bed around 7:30."

As Gina was walking towards the door, her mom said, "The yellow looks great on you! And don't worry about us at all. We'll be fine. You just worry about you and have fun!"

Gina smiled back at her mom just before she closed the door. "Oh, we will. I'll tell you all about it when I get home."

Her mom gave her a serious look. "You better. I'm not watching this little monster for nothing!" She looked at Nathan. "Right, little guy. Your mom better hold up her end of the bargain!"

"Don't worry, Mom. I'll tell you all about it later," she promised as she closed the door.

* * * * * * * * * *

About forty-five minutes later, Gina arrived in Moose Lake, the designated meeting spot. They had picked it not only because it was midway between their two cities, but because it would provide them with some anonymity. They didn't want any idle tongues spreading rumors, so they purposely avoided meeting in either of their hometowns. She quickly found the Subway, which wasn't too difficult a feat because of the size of the town.

As she got out of her car, she looked around the parking lot and saw Brett getting out of his vehicle a few cars down from hers. He didn't see her yet, so she took the opportunity to get a good look at him. He was looking rather handsome in his white shirt with red and blue pinstripes. She couldn't help but smile.

Eventually he noticed Gina and returned the smile. "Hey. Fancy meeting you here."

"Yeah, what a coincidence...both of us showing up at the same time," she said jokingly.

He came to her side and hooked his elbow in hers. "It's like we planned it or something." Then he looked over at her and said, "Yellow is a good color on you. You look beautiful."

Gina blushed. "Thanks," she managed to say. "You are looking rather dapper yourself in your pinstripes."

"I kind of feel like a sailor," he said.

"Well, as long as you don't drink or swear like a sailor, I'll be seen with you in public," Gina teased.

He laughed. "Well, I don't drink. And I honestly don't remember the last time I swore, so I think we'll be fine." He cleared his throat and gestured to the Subway. "Sorry about the restaurant choice. They don't really have any nice places to eat here, so I figured Subway was as good a place as any. Besides, I really like their meatball subs."

Gina shrugged her shoulders. "Subway is fine. It's probably one of my favorite places to eat, if truth be told. So nice work picking out the restaurant."

"Hey, thanks. I try. And I hope you don't mind meeting in Moose Lake. I know it's kind of small, but it is right in the middle of us." He leaned in conspiratorially. "I think I told you this, but I grew up around this area. So it's kind of like coming home for me in a way."

"Hmm," she said thoughtfully. "I think you may have mentioned it in one of our phone calls. Did you like growing up here?" she asked him.

He seemed to consider her question for a moment before answering. "Overall, yes. Sometimes I wished it was a little bit bigger so there was more to do, but I liked growing up in a small town overall. There's just something about small town people." He opened the door for her and whispered as she went in, "Though I am hoping I don't run into any of those fine small town people today. I don't think we need any tattling toadies spreading rumors out there."

As they got in line, the guy in front of them turned around and did a double-take at Brett. "Brett Johnson?" he said.

Brett smiled good-naturedly and stuck out his hand. "Mike. Long time, no see," he said as the two of them shook hands. "What have you been up to?"

"Ah, you know, the usual. Work, work, and more work. In fact, I just got off a long shift and stopped by for something to eat. How about you?"

"I'm still teaching. That keeps me busy. Track will be starting up soon, so that will keep me out of trouble before summer."

"Yeah, you were always one for getting into tons of trouble," Mike said sarcastically. "Anyway, how many years has it been since we've seen each other?" Mike asked.

Brett thought about it before answering. "Probably about four years. I think it was at our last class reunion."

The two guys chit-chatted a little in line, and after Brett and Gina got their subs and found a table, Brett whispered to Gina, "So much for not running into anyone I know."

Gina laughed. "Yeah, so much for that. Oh, well. He doesn't seem like he's the type to go blab it all over or anything."

Brett seemed to consider this. "True, true. I think you have Mike figured out." He cleared his throat. "Do you mind if I pray for the food?" he asked.

"No, not at all," Gina said.

The two bowed their heads and Brett said, "God, thank you so much for bringing Gina here tonight. Also, thank you so much for our food and our many blessings. You have been so faithful to both of us during our hard times, and we are so grateful for that. Amen."

"Amen," Gina said as she looked up at Brett. As he had voiced in his prayer, she was extremely thankful that God had helped them both through their hard times, and she felt a swell of gratitude towards God for bringing the two of them together in the midst of it all. *He works all things for the good of those who love Him*, she thought to herself as the two of them started to eat their subs.

* * * * * * * * *

A few hours later, Gina opened the door to her house and bustled in, extremely tired but giddy with excitement after an eventful evening out. She saw her mom on the living room couch reading a magazine.

"Hey, honey," her mom said, instantly putting her magazine down. "Well, there's certainly no hiding that huge smile on your face. I take it that it went well."

Gina flopped on the couch. "Yeah, it did. We had a lot of fun."

"Details. I need details," her mom prodded.

"Well, he was wearing a white shirt with pinstripes and he looked really cute. And he liked my yellow shirt. Good pick, mom."

Her mom smiled smugly. "I knew he would like it. What did you two do all evening?"

"Well, we met at Subway. There aren't really many restaurants in Moose Lake. Anyway, we talked for a while there and then went to this place called Hanging Horn Village, which isn't really much of a village at all, but it does have a restaurant with excellent food. We went into the restaurant and talked for a while, and then decided we needed some ice cream. So then we went to Dairy Queen and had Blizzards. After that, the Dairy Queen was closing but we both weren't ready for our evening to be over, so we went back to Subway and talked for about an hour. Then I came home," she said airily. "And here I am."

"Yes, and here you are. That sounds like a lot of eating and talking. You must be really full after all of that," her mom teased.

Gina put one of her hands on her stomach. "Yeah. I am really full."

"So I take it there will be a second date?" her mom said.

Gina gave her a look. "Yes, there will be a second *outing*," she said pointedly.

Her mom rolled her eyes. "Oh, sorry. *Outing*, I meant." She put her hands on her hips. "When are you two going to just call it what it is? Dating. That's what you're doing, whether you call it that or not."

Gina gave her mom a helpless look. "Mom, it's kind of complicated, especially on his end. I mean, on my end, Drew died almost a year ago, so most people would think it was acceptable if we were dating, but on his end, Kara died just four months ago. Some people, especially her family, might feel like he didn't really care about her if he started dating someone else, though we all know that isn't the case. He still misses her deeply. We both talk about it all of the time." She sighed and ran her hands through her brown curls. "It's just so... complicated. Ugh!"

Her mom reached across the couch and gave her a hug. "I know it is, honey. Life is never as easy as we would like it to be."

Gina let her mom hug her for a while before breaking away. "We are just going to take it slowly and just see how it all goes. We aren't in a hurry or anything."

Her mom reached over and grabbed her hand. "God's in control of all of it anyway. Plus, you have a lot of people praying for you."

Gina smiled gratefully at her mom. "I know, Mom." She paused for a moment and then looked back over at her mom. "Mom?"

"Yeah?"

"Thanks. You really are the best."

Her mom's eyes moistened a bit and then she said, "And don't you forget it!"

CHAPTER TWENTY-ONE

Brett

The past three months had flown by in a flurry of emails, phone calls, and dates with Gina. Shortly after their first outing in Moose Lake, the two had decided that they would just admit that they were dating and start calling it "what it was," as Gina's mother had so bluntly put it. The two of them answered to God, not people, and they both felt like it was God's will that they were together in the first place.

But it was still rather complicated. Brett himself had a difficult time fathoming how he could be grieving the loss of Kara, but still feel excited about the prospect of dating Gina. He felt that he loved them both. It didn't lessen his love for Kara because he was beginning to love Gina. In fact, it was quite the opposite. It was as if he had been given a greater capacity to love. He figured it was kind of like when you had a child. Before you have the child, you have a hard time believing that it's possible to love someone else as much as your spouse, but then it happens, and you just do. Love somehow multiplies right before your eyes.

And he did really love Gina. There were just so many things he loved about her. First and foremost, she had a rock-solid faith that was evident to anyone she came in contact with. She was a natural beauty inside and out, radiating God's love to everyone around her. She was also incredibly caring, especially with Nathan and Grant. He felt she loved Brett for who he was, and that was important to him. To top it off, she was just plain fun to be around. She had taught him that he could truly live life again, with an unbridled passion for God and others.

He completely felt at peace with dating Gina, but not everyone else was, particularly Kara's parents. It was something that continually weighed on his mind. After bringing up Gina at Christmas, he hadn't dared to broach the topic again. But he felt that it was time.

Since he wasn't sure he could adequately express what he wanted to say in words, he decided to write it in a letter. That way, he could type and delete, getting his words exactly as he wanted them before sending the letter off. After many versions, he decided to send the following letter off to them:

April 28, 2006

William and Martha,

I wanted to write this letter to you for two different reasons. I hope putting these reasons into words will solidify their significance, both for me and for you.

The first reason for this letter is to allow me a chance to put into words, to the best of my ability, my emotions and desires for our future. It goes without saying that this process has been a difficult one. Yet, I can't say enough that I feel so blessed to have you to as my in-laws during this time. Your encouragement, prayers, and support have made this difficult time more bearable. Kara respected and loved you guys so much and there is nothing I could ever do or say to adequately communicate that to you. As the years have passed since I first met you, I have grown to feel the same way she did. You two are, and always will be, my second parents, and I value your godly influence and character. Because of this, and obviously because of Kara, I want you to be a part of Grant's and my life forever. You will be the best avenue for Grant to get to know Kara. Rest assured, I will no doubt do my best as well, but nothing can replace a parent's treasure-trove of stories, reactions, and feelings. Life without you two would be much more difficult and unfathomable.

The second reason I'm writing this is to begin a conversation with you about Gina and me. The three of us have not actively discussed Gina's and my relationship lately. I would like for us to begin that dialogue. I do not have the ability to understand how difficult this may be for you, and up to this point I have not ever brought up the topic of dating her out of respect for your feelings. Please know that I am not intending to be insensitive by bringing it up now. However, as much as a paradox as it might seem, I feel that, out of respect for our future relationship, I must bring this topic up now.

It still does not make much sense to me how the following can be the case: loving someone new while grieving for a lost spouse. However, in reality, it is happening right now. As I said before, the grief and loneliness I have felt (and will continue to feel) at times is overwhelming. At the same time, it is not my personality, nor do I believe it is God's will for me, to wallow in that grief. The Lord's will is that I move on with this temporal life. When I say move on, I do NOT mean forget. I have no doubt in my mind that God has given me this relationship with Gina for a long-term purpose. God knows that I need someone to care for me, just as Kara did. She would often say that I would be in a world of trouble if I ever had to manage the whole household, especially with Grant on top of it all. God also knows the following about this relationship: 1) Grant and I need someone to care for us. 2) Grant and I need a woman to love. 3) Gina and Nathan need someone to care for them. 4) Gina and Nathan need a man to love. Both Gina and I feel that this is God's will, and so do numerous others who are close to us. In fact, none of our close friends have come up to either one of us to say that they think that we are in the wrong.

One thing I can say for sure is this: God is answering our prayers, because I feel them through my relationship with Gina. In fact, I've heard people say, "Brett's doing so well considering what he's gone through," and from the outside, it may seem that way. What everyone does not see is exactly how that's happening. First, it has nothing to do with me. It is entirely God working through me, carrying me, and most importantly, providing for me! He has used so many people to help me manage my life: you and my parents, my Mora family, and all that Kara has built into my life.

Gina has also been a huge part of that. I will emphatically say that there is no way that I would have been able to keep my head up during the really tough times I've been through since December without Gina. That statement has huge repercussions, not only for me, but for Grant. What kind of dad would I be to him if all I could do was mope around, frustrated and mad at the stresses of life, depressed and forlorn because I'm living alone? I believe that that environment would not be in his best interest.

Another comment I want to add to this letter is actually something that my mom pointed out to me. My mom had come down to watch Grant, and, after he had gone to bed, I just needed to relax and talk about some stuff on my mind, specifically memories of when Grant was born. As we were talking and reminiscing, we recalled how very close Kara was to having a c-section with Grant. Then she made a comment that will probably resonate in my mind forever: "We can really praise God for the time Kara was with us, especially after Grant was born. What would have happened had Grant been born through a c-section? She could have gotten that air bubble into her system right there in the delivery room and passed away!"

WOW! There have not been many things in my past that have so radically changed my point of view than this. I am so blessed to have had Kara as my wife. It was at that point where I really decided that I had to do the following IMMEDIATELY: 1) I have to give my grief up to God. 2) I have to be completely and utterly in awe of his will, provision, and wisdom. 3) I have to look back on all of the days I had with Kara, especially since Grant was born, and smile laugh, and truly cherish them. I thought of them as so very precious before, but now thinking about how they might never have been if she had died giving birth, I'm entirely speechless. 4) I have to trust God with everything in my future.

Please understand that I will never be done grieving. Although it may seem like I have moved on from an outward perspective, I know that I will be missing and loving Kara for the rest of my life. She was my first true love. God literally used her to teach me how to be a godly man and how to love not just her, but also others around me. She taught me to come out of my shell and communicate, rather than keep so many feelings and emotions inside. Besides the fact that the timing with Grant seemed horrible, it also felt like this timing couldn't have been worse for our marriage. Kara and I were really starting to jive and connect. The learning curve was steep for this stubborn Finn for the first few years of our marriage. In fact, at a recent track and field meet I attended while coaching, a parent was surprised to learn that we shared a Finnish heritage. She commented that this was too unbelievable because I was just too open and outgoing to be a Finn-lander. I paused for a second to consider her comment. I had never thought of that before. Without much more than that, I replied that teaching has helped some, but what helped the most was being married to Kara. She taught me how to love, communicate, and see the importance of thinking outside of my own mind. We had worked

through so many issues that had come out for the
better in the end.

I'm sorry if this seems disjointed as I weave
from Kara to Gina to Kara again. The only thing that
I can say is that this is how I foresee life being
in the future: me deeply loving and respecting them
both. I never thought it would be possible to love
two people, but God is making it happen.

I want to include another thought about how Gina
has really helped me to grieve. Both of you have
your best friend and soul-mate to confide in during
this time. You can sit down with one another and
share memories of Kara that both of you remember.
You can talk about how you remember trips, school
programs, and other details from her life. I don't
have that luxury. I don't have anyone to share
stories with.

Well, at least I didn't. However, as my
relationship with Gina grew, it occurred to me that
this relationship was helping me so incredibly much
and I didn't even realize it. As Gina and I told
each other stories about Andy and Kara, not only was
the other person getting to know them, but also the
person sharing was reliving the memory of them. And
since neither of us knew the other's spouses prior
to sharing, we each had to explain all the minute
details that go with those special memories. For
example, I'm not going to tell a family member about
the nuances of Kara's life and personality; the
family member would already know. But Gina doesn't.
She's getting to know Kara as I tell these stories,
and I'm getting to know Andy as she talks to me.
The more those stories and nuances are discussed,
the grief subsides and the memories are cemented
in our minds. What a huge blessing!

Both you and Gina are a huge part of my life. I
know that you are not going away or disappearing
from my life or Grant's. Gina, too, is not going

away; in fact, our relationship is progressing. Being emotionally pulled like this is difficult (I never expected it to be easy). You are missing a piece of my life and as that piece grows and grows, it becomes harder and harder for me to be in the middle. I'll be honest because I feel torn between what I feel is God's will for me and your grief. (And please, please don't take this as a guilt trip. It is definitely not that!) Based on this fact and the advice of two pastors at our church, I need and want to provide you with opportunities to meet Gina and begin developing that relationship. I say "need" for the reasons I just stated and I say "want" because I'm so excited for you two to meet her. She is also very excited to meet you.

The first opportunity for this will be at Grant's upcoming birthday party. My prayer for you is that in the next couple of weeks, you will grow to understand a piece of my life and be willing to meet Gina at Grant's party. I do realize that the party will be hard enough as it is, so if you'd rather, you are welcome to stay overnight on Friday and/or Saturday night. Gina would also be willing to stay over those nights and you could spend time getting to know her then rather than on a day of significance. I'm open to other suggestions, too, if you have any, so we can make this transition as smooth as possible.

I do know that I cannot reason with your emotions, so please do not read this as a letter to convince you that your are wrong in any way. For Grant's and my sake, along with all of our futures, I needed to type this letter to share what was on my heart. I love you two!

Sincerely,

Your son, Brett

After addressing the envelope and putting a stamp on it, Brett brought it to the mailbox and put the flag up. He silently said a prayer for God to help them on their end as they read the letter.

He wasn't sure how they were going to react, but he was sure of one thing: He loved Gina and she loved him back. She wasn't going to go away, no matter what their reaction was. In fact, Brett had recently been looking at rings and felt that he would ask the big question soon. Though he wasn't sure what Kara's parents would think of that, he did know in his heart of hearts that it was the right thing for him, for Gina, and for the two boys. And for that, he couldn't wait.

* * * * * * * * * *

A few weeks later, Brett called one of his good friends, Jim, to meet for lunch. The lunch outing had a dual purpose. First and foremost, he hadn't seen Jim for a while and he wanted to catch up with him. Also, he needed someone to give him advice, and he trusted Jim more than almost anyone in that area. Jim had not only been his friend for years, but he was also a pastor and had a rock-solid faith in God. The latter made Jim's advice even more reliable in Brett's eyes. Not only that, but Jim had been with him through the worst. While in the hospital, Jim was one of the people who had visited often and had walked Brett through the doors away from Kara when the doctors unplugged her from the machines. To put it simply, Jim was there when he needed a friend the most.

As he pushed the door open to Pizza Hut, he saw Jim in the corner booth. Jim was a booth kind of guy, so Brett had known exactly where to look. Brett waved and walked over to his friend, who stood up and engulfed Brett in a huge bear hug.

"How are you, man?" Jim said upon releasing Brett.

Brett smiled. "I'm surviving. One day at a time."

Jim returned the smile. "Surviving? More like thriving! You amaze me, my friend. I'm pretty sure that I would still be in bed with the covers over my head if I was in your situation."

Brett laughed at Jim's candor. "Well, if I'm being completely honest, there are days where I am tempted to do just that. But then Grant cries and I am forced to get my feet on the floor. Necessity trumps emotion."

Jim, a father of two himself, laughed sympathetically. "Yes, I can relate. Kids are not conducive to sleep. Or free time. Or anytime for anyone else whatsoever." He raised his eyebrows. "Though you have found some time for your new lady friend from what you've told me. I am impressed."

Brett grimaced as he sat down in the booth across from Jim. "Yeah, that I have. But it's definitely a long story. And very complicated. We'll talk more about that after we order our pizza."

"Life always is, my man. Let's get our pizza ordered and then discuss the lady friend." As the two scoured the menu, Jim said, "So what are you thinking? About the pizza, I mean. Not the lady friend."

Brett smiled. Jim could always put a smile on his face. "I'm up for anything. What looks good to you?"

Jim hit his chest and deepened his voice. "I'm thinking meat. And lots of it."

Brett laughed. "So...meat lover's it is. Sounds good to me."

After the waitress brought their beverages and they placed their order, Jim said, "Okay, lay it on me. I'm ready."

Brett sighed. He figured he should just catch Jim up the fastest way he knew how, so he said, "Well...I bought a ring."

Jim's eyebrows shot up pretty quickly. "Wow. So it's that serious. Have you asked her yet?"

Brett shook his head. "No, not yet. But I did talk to Gina's parents to ask permission and I talked to Kara's parents, as well."

Jim's eyes widened. "So, how did that go over?"

Brett cleared his throat and leaned back in the booth. "Well, Gina's parents seemed pretty excited about it all."

Jim cocked an eyebrow. "And Kara's?"

"That's where it gets complicated," Brett admitted.

"I was almost afraid to ask, but I had to. Tell me about it," Jim prodded.

Brett sighed. "Well, you already know about the letter I wrote to William and Martha, right?"

Jim nodded. "You told me about that the last time we talked. I remember that you were careful to both declare your undying love for Kara and your growing love for Gina. Am I remembering correctly?"

"Exactly," Brett said, impressed at Jim's attention to detail. "I thought that the letter might have softened their hearts to any further developments with Gina, but I guess I was wrong."

Jim leaned forward, his gaze intensifying at this revelation. "How so? You mean they weren't happy for you and Gina?"

Brett shrugged his shoulders. "I think they were *trying* to be happy for us, but they couldn't mask the displeasure in their voices. They said it was too soon. They hinted that they thought I was replacing Kara with Gina, which I'm not. I will never be able to replace their daughter. I will always love her." Brett's voice caught and he looked down at his wedding band, which he still wore and planned on wearing for a very long time.

After a moment of silence, Jim said, "Hey. Look at me."

Brett looked up as Jim spoke. "You haven't done anything wrong. They just need some time. They are still holding on to Kara as tightly as they can, where you have released her to Jesus. Everyone grieves differently. And everyone who knows you well knows that you loved Kara and will always love her. Just because you also happen to love someone else right now doesn't diminish your love for Kara."

Brett hadn't realized that he was holding his breath as Jim spoke, and he slowly released it now. "That's exactly how I feel." He looked out the window, collecting his thoughts. "I used to think that human beings were given only a certain capacity to love. I married Kara, and I thought that I would never be able to love someone as much as I loved her. Then we had baby Grant. It was then that I realized that our capacity to love somehow multiplies the longer we live. I didn't love Kara any less because I loved Grant. In fact, it was the opposite. I almost loved Kara more because of my love for Grant." He paused for a moment and then continued on. "And now with Gina, my love for her has in no way diminished my love for Kara. I talk about Kara often with Gina, and somehow, my love for both of them has increased. It's hard to explain."

Jim smiled. "That's because love is a God thing." He looked right at Brett and continued. "I've been praying for you daily, and once you met Gina, I started praying for both of you. I know that both of you love God and have kept Him in the center of all of this, so if you feel ready to marry her, then I know that the timing is right. You have to trust that it is right, too."

Brett ran his hand through his hair. "I know. I do truly feel like it's right and that it's God's will for us. I've spoken with Pastor Jerry, some of my other close friends, and Gina has spoken to her closest friends. Everyone who knows us well agrees that the timing is right... except for Kara's parents. But that makes it so...complicated." A huge sigh escaped from Brett as he said the last word.

Jim reached across the table put an encouraging hand on Brett's forearm. "I know it's complicated, buddy. But if you believe that God feels it's right, that you and Gina feel it's right, and that those closest to you feel that it's right...then you just need to forge ahead with it. Life's too short to wait on what you feel is God's best for you."

As Brett took a bite of his pizza, he chewed on Jim's words. "I know. It's just easy to dwell on the naysayers sometimes. And there are plenty of those out there. Apparently, there are some people around town who feel like our relationship has developed too quickly, as well."

Jim gave him a quizzical look. "Anyone you know well?"

Brett shook his head. "No. Just people around town."

"Ah. You can't listen to them." He gestured dismissively. "You can never let people who don't know the whole story keep you from pursuing what you feel is God's will."

Brett had a glimmer of a smile beginning. "You're right. I mean, I felt all of these things even before I spoke to you, but it sure helps to hear you say them."

Jim smiled warmly. "That's why I'm here, buddy." His eyes twinkled. "And next time I hear from you, you better have some big news to tell me."

Brett felt his smile broaden. "I will. Don't worry, I will."

"Good," Jim said. "Now I know you already started eating, but I'd like to say a prayer for your future. And the food. In that order."

Brett laughed. "Sounds good. No objections from me."

As the two bowed their heads in prayer, Brett felt more at peace than he had in a long time. He surely would have big news for his friend the next time he saw him.

CHAPTER TWENTY-TWO

Gina

"**M**om! Guess what!" Gina practically screamed into the phone.

"Honey! What is it?"

"I'm officially engaged! Can you believe it?" Gina said excitedly into the phone.

Her mom squealed. "I knew it. I just knew it. I said to your father just the other day, 'Honey, the next time Gina calls, I think she's going to have some big news for us.' And now you do. Congratulations, honey. I couldn't be more happy for you two!"

"Thanks, Mom. I knew you would be excited. I just can't believe it's actually happening! It seems like it's all happened so fast, but at the same time, I feel like I've known Brett for longer than I have. He's just so great, Mom."

"Yes, he sure is. And now Nathan will have a daddy, just like you prayed for," her mom reminded her.

Gina smiled on her end of the phone. "Yes, Mom, you're exactly right. I prayed for a daddy for Nathan before he turned two, and God answered my prayer, even though I thought it would be nearly impossible when I was praying it."

"Well, there were a lot of prayers going up for you, honey. God probably just decided to answer the prayers to keep us all quiet," her mom joked.

"I am so thankful to have a family like ours," Gina said. "You are all so supportive and always have been."

"No problem, sweetie. That's why we're here." Her mom paused on the other end of the phone, and Gina assumed she was probably getting all teary-eyed. "Enough of this mushy-mushy stuff. Let's get down to the details. How did he ask you to marry him? Do you two have a date picked out? Any wedding ideas? This is all just so exciting!"

Gina laughed. "Oh, Mom. I love how excited you are right now. Anyway, here's how he asked me. I've told you about geocaching before, right? You know, where there are hidden objects and you are given clues, and you have to go around looking for them?"

"Yes, I vaguely remember you explaining this to me before."

"Well, the two of us both like geocaching, so on Saturday, we went out looking for an object with our clues, but when we found the object, it was actually the ring. Then, right then and there, he got down on one knee to ask me to marry him. We were in the middle of nowhere with a patch of woods, a little stream, and nature all around us."

"Oh, how romantic," her mom swooned. "And very creative. I love it!" She paused for a moment. "And have you picked a date? I want to get it on my calendar right now!"

"Well, I know this is only two months away, but we are thinking the first weekend in August. And don't freak out, Mom, because we are just going to do a small, casual wedding with family and close friends. We were actually thinking of asking Grandma and Grandpa if we could have it at their house on Grindstone Lake. It's a beautiful spot and it would be perfect for a small and personal wedding."

"Oh, I'm sure they would love to have it. It would be so beautiful right on the lake!" her mom said.

"So you don't think it's bad if we don't have it in a church? And that it's not a big wedding?" Gina asked.

"Oh, no, not at all." Her mom paused, as if weighing her words. "Gina, this is your second wedding. You've already had the big church wedding before. You are at a different point in your life now, and you should do it exactly the way you two see fit. People will just be so happy for you two, and they won't care if it's not the typical wedding setting."

Gina exhaled the breath she had been holding. "You have no idea how glad I am that you just said that, Mom. Brett and I really want to keep it small and very casual, but we also want to be respectful of those we love most. It just means a lot to hear you say that people will be happy for us no matter what."

"I'd fly to the Arctic Circle if that's where you were having the wedding, honey. And so would any of our family and your close friends. We have all been pulling for you over the past year, Gina, and we couldn't be happier." Her mom paused for a moment on her end of the phone, as if thinking. "Besides, I think people will just be excited to hear some good news for once. This world is full enough of bad news. It almost makes me not want to watch the news anymore. But this, my dear, is the best news I've heard in a while. In fact, I don't know what I'll do with myself over the next two months. I'm just so excited."

Gina laughed. Her mother was one-of-a-kind. "Well, I have a pretty good idea what you'll be doing, Mom. Helping me with the wedding plans! We only have two months!"

"Oh, goody! I love planning events. And I do work well with a deadline!" her mom said, matching Gina's laugh with her own.

* * * * * * * * *

Two months later, on August 6th, Gina found herself joining hands and locking eyes with Brett while standing in front of the pastor in her grandparents' backyard, surrounded by their immediate family and a few close friends. She'd had to pinch herself multiple times that day to reassure herself that it was actually happening and wasn't just a dream, and sure enough, the day had finally come. She flashed Brett a huge smile, so excited for their future, and he squeezed her hand and smiled back.

The two had made it a casual affair, with Brett donning khaki shorts with a short-sleeved dress shirt and Gina wearing a sundress. The meal to come would be backyard picnic style, low-stress and hopefully conversation-inducing.

As the pastor was about to start on the vows, a fisherman trolled by and waved at them. Both of them saw it simultaneously, looked at each other, and giggled. Gina couldn't help but think that it just added to the ambiance of the whole day.

Brett and Gina had made it a priority to honor their first spouses and their families in the wedding ceremony. In addition to the unity candle the two had chosen, they also had the unity candles from each of their first weddings. They used the flames of those candles to light the flame of their new unity candle. Once the new unity candle was lit, the flames from the prior unity candles were extinguished, symbolizing how the love and influence from their first spouses were being transferred into this new marriage and would always be a part of them. Also, they had both made the decision to wear the wedding bands from their first weddings to the wedding and all the days thereafter. In addition, they had roses for Andy's and Kara's mothers at the ceremony, which were given to them while the song "Love Alone" by Caedmon's Call played softly in the background, the line, "Give me Your hand to hold 'cause I can't stand to love alone," setting the ambiance for that moment.

Later, after the meal was over and everyone sat contentedly full, chatting with their loved ones around them, Gina saw one of the handouts that she and Brett had given out to each of their guests. It told their story from each of their perspectives. Brett's was first, and he told about Gina's first letter of encouragement and how things had progressed from there, ending with what he loved about Gina. Then Gina's version of their story started, and as Gina picked up the handout, she silently marveled at how God had brought the two of them together. She read the words she had typed a few days earlier:

```
"Praise be to the God and Father of our Lord Jesus
Christ, the Father of compassion and the God of all
comfort, who comforts us in all our troubles, so
that we can comfort those in any trouble with the
comfort that we ourselves have received from God."
(2 Corinthians 1:3-4)
    This is the verse that prompted me to write a
note of encouragement to Brett. I knew first-hand
how hard it was to lose a spouse and also to be a
single parent of a baby. It's such a difficult spot
to be in, and it certainly doesn't seem fair that
a loving God would do this. I found quickly that
there are so few people that are in a spot like
ours, so I wanted to reach out to tell Brett that
God is loving. He just needed to wait and see...God
would come through for him. I also wanted to let
```

him know that there was someone else out there in a similar situation and that he was not alone.

Since you are here at our wedding reception, you obviously know the culmination of the story already. What started as an encouragement note progressed to phone calls, cross-country skiing, dating, and then growing to love one another. It wasn't just the loss of a spouse that we had in common, but found so much more in each other that we love. God has used each of us to help heal the other. After Andy died, I knew that I would want to get married again and to find a companion for myself and a daddy for Nathan. I just didn't know if I had the emotional capacity to do that. God has been so faithful in doing more than I could ask or even imagine. God provided someone for me who completely understood my pain and struggles and would listen to me cry. Not only has God provided a new "best friend" for me, but also someone I enjoy so many things with and feel safe confiding in. God has proven over and over again in big and small ways that He is in control and that He loves and cares for me in just the ways that I need it.

I know people will ask, "How do you know that he's the one?" There is no special divine revelation or sign; when you know, you know! I had been married before and I knew what I was looking for and what I wanted. So it didn't take me long to get this one figured out. I had been praying that God would provide someone for me to love and someone to love Nathan and me. All throughout our dating relationship I kept questioning God because it all just seemed too good to be true. I questioned that God really could provide something this incredible! At times I just look at Brett in bewilderment because all of this is so amazing. God really does make things that seem too good to be true TRUE! There are so many little things about Brett that I love: his sense of humor (both laughing with me and at me), his taste in music, ways he likes to have fun, his adventurousness, and many more things. What I love the most about Brett is first and foremost his desire for God. He has a passion to live how God wants him to live and really takes it to heart when he knows what God is talking to him about. Spiritual accountability is something that I need, and God has provided that for me through Brett.

Brett is kind in so many ways. This is shown in opening doors for me, taking out my trash, giving me a hug when I'm having a hard time, or just looking at me and asking, "Are you okay?" He is also just plain fun to be with. We love to play with each other. Whether it is cribbage, ping pong, skiing, running, water fights, or rock skipping, we are bound to be smiling and laughing. Being together isn't work; it just flows. I've been lucky enough to find someone I just can't get enough of.

Brett has taken the role of caregiver in our relationship. It feels so good to have someone to care for me. He not only cares for the logistics of life, but for my emotional needs, too. That is shown in just holding my hand, or, at times, holding all of me. He understands what it is to grieve and allows me to do that. He is not offended that I love two men at once, both him and Andy. We both understand that we will always love our first spouse, but God has also given us the capacity to love another. How amazing is God that He has provided just what we needed and desired. We didn't try to make this happen...it just happened. God made it happen.

-Gina

Epilogue

Since getting married, life has been quite the adventure for the Johnson's. They have weathered raising two boys, moving from a house in town to the country, getting a dog, raising puppies from that dog, and, just when the two thought they had everything under control, God brought them a new little bundle of joy in the form of a third boy (surprise!), whom they named Trent. Life may not always be easy, but it is always an adventure.

There have also been some recent developments in Brett and Gina's relationship with Kara's parents, which had been strained for years. Through godly advice from their pastors and through a process called "peacemaking" where both parties meet with a Christian counselor with the goal of understanding each other, and, ultimately, forgiveness, huge breakthroughs have been made in repairing that relationship. Through the process, Brett and Gina realized more fully that the hurt went both ways and that the two of them needed to take some of the responsibility for what had transpired. In essence, we are all flawed creatures and need to ask for forgiveness. Blaming doesn't solve anything, even if it seems warranted to some degree. God forgave us freely, and so must we forgive. If we are willing to do that, then it leaves the door open for God to work miracles in what may seem like a hopeless situation.

It is my hope, as the author, and the Johnson's hope, that you have seen how God never leaves or forsakes any of us. He brings HOPE to the hopeless, LOVE to the hurting, and HELP to those who ask for it. Bring your burdens and pain to Him, for He cares so much for you. Give God a chance. Though we may not always understand His ways or His timing, He is always faithful. Even if it is The Long Way Around, He always comes around to those who seek Him.

A note from "Gina" a.k.a Kristy:

This book is not just a cute love story; it's more than that. It is the story of redemption. Broken relationships and wounds were healed by the One who has the power to do it.

Both Brett and Gina lost their spouses, but they also lost the dreams they had with those spouses. The day their spouses died, those dreams were lost also. You may smile to think that they found love again in another spouse, but that spouse will never hold their hand like Andy or Kara would have. Brett will never tease Gina like Andy did and Gina will never hug Brett like Kara did. The type of relationship may have been replaced, but the person never will be replaced.

Not only did Brett and Gina lose a spouse, but the present absence of Andy and Kara leaves a hole in their parents' hearts. The loss of a child can't be replaced for a parent. There are times where this reality and deep suffering is not overcome here on earth. But someday in eternity, these broken relationships will be restored and the tears will be wiped away and never return. This deep suffering and each of our own quests to process it, deal with it, and struggle to move on can cause clashes in relationships.

The relationship between Brett/Gina and William/Martha was strained for a long, long time. It was not the fault of just one person, but the clash of everyone, struggling in their own way to move on in life after a deep heartache. What ultimately brought healing to their own hearts individually and also to their relationship? It was God. It is a profound mystery how God can work so gently, yet firmly when He has access to a humble heart of a person who is willing to let Him shine the light into dark places and flood the heart with healing. Brokenness doesn't always have to wait until heaven to be healed. Sometimes it can be healed here on earth. No relationship was ever healed while sitting in a pool of bitterness. Relationships are healed with humbleness, openness, and forgiveness. Brett, Gina, William and Martha have all done the hard work of that. Their relationship is better now than it ever has been. There is such freedom in forgiveness. This is available to you, reader, also, for your broken relationships.

The past emotions are gone for Brett, Gina, William and Martha, and what is left is a heart that is full of gratitude for a God who can make all things new.

"Moreover, I will give you a new heart and put a new spirit within you; and I will remove the heart of stone from your flesh." -Ezekiel 36:26

-Kristy

A note from "Brett" a.k.a. Derek:

Thanks for reading this slightly fictionalized version of my and Kristy's ("Gina's") love story. I would now like to be transparent with you about how I handled this grief and then challenge you to consider being a part of something bigger than yourself.

When I think of that time after Karlynn ("Kara") died, there were many family and friends who held me up when I wanted to fall. There were also many words (i.e. the Bible) that kept me upright, but I'd like to highlight one in particular: **LIFE.** I know this seems like an oxymoron, and you may wonder, "In the midst of death, how can you be thinking of life?"

To begin with, I was forced to look life in the eyes every day when Grant woke up. A five-and-a-half-month old doesn't understand death; he just knows he pooped his pants and he's hungry. There's no doubt that, in human terms, he was my ultimate grief-coping mechanism.

Beyond that, more sacred definitions of life gave me great comfort during that time. First and most importantly, Karlynn had a deep faith in Jesus. Through all of the ups and downs we experienced together, she never wavered. This includes the last two months of her life, when she had every reason to fall apart. In fact, it was during those days when I was most impressed with her faith.

After her death, I was comforted by the fact that she was in the presence of our eternal King, Jesus. She had true life and it would never end. Jesus had given Karlynn life and that life would never be taken away from her again.

Secondly, Karlynn had chosen to be an organ, eye, and tissue donor. She gave the ultimate gift: **LIFE.** It was because of her that five others were able to live, and live not just a so-so kind of life, but one of adventure. Her parents received a letter from one of the recipients, informing them that he was now able to get back outdoors and do the things he loved. Karlynn loved the outdoors, too! Karlynn had given life to a stranger she would never meet.

We all have these two choices in front of us today: faith and life. Both of these choices are free for all of us to make

Despite the condition of your life, when you surrender and walk in faith, Jesus will heal you and give you eternal life.

Despite the condition of your body, you can be an organ, eye, and tissue donor (There are very few absolute restrictions and no strict upper or lower age limits*) and extend someone's life.

The need for donors is so real and urgent: every day 21 people die because of the shortage of organs, eyes, and tissue and a new person is added to the donor waiting list every 10 minutes**. Your generosity will not only impact the recipient and his/her family, your heart-broken family will also be encouraged.

Humor me for a moment and consider a question (even if you are young and feel invincible): What will your family and friends feel when you die, especially if it's sudden like Karlynn's was? I know that's a morbid and narcissistic thought, but it has a purpose so hang in there and keep reading.

If you've lost someone close, you know a little of what it's like. It's emotionally overwhelming, physically exhausting, and can be spiritually crippling. Your family will be feeling this, too. Their heads will be spinning and just getting out of bed will require concentrated effort. Never mind eating, working, laundry, home maintenance, and paying bills. Losing you has now become their full-time job.

After everyone has gone home and returned to "normal," your family will be at their deepest point of grief. It's at this moment when they will receive a package in the mail, and it won't be another "I'm so sorry for your loss" floral shop greeting card.

This package instead will be filled with compassion, honor, and gratitude. It will tell your family that your death has allowed someone else to live. Your family will read the age of a person who has been waiting in fear of impending death. This letter will describe to your loved ones how, in such a short period of time, this unknown person now has the chance to live a life that was only a dream just a few short weeks prior. Your family will have a real connection to this person. Your family will feel as if a piece of you is still seeking adventure, still changing the world, because it is. This will give them hope that no mountain of cards and garden of flowers can.

I can speak from experience: it makes all the difference in the world. The questions of "WHY DID THIS HAPPEN?" and "HOW CAN I LIVE LIFE?" won't hold the sting and bitterness that it did initially. The clenched fist will begin to open, the tear-filled eyes will begin to clear, and the broken heart . . . well, it will still hurt, but the knowledge of another family being spared from what they are feeling really does help. And even years after Karlynn's death, I can pick up the phone and call LifeSource (Minnesota's procurement organization) and they will be there to listen to and support me.

Becoming a donor is very easy. When you renew your driver's license, check the "DONOR" box. But you don't have to wait; you can register right now. Just visit http://donatelifeamerica.org/, click "Register now," find your state, and sign up. But don't stop there. It's important to share your decision with your family or loved ones so they also know of your wishes.

Registering to be a donor is a very personal and important decision so if you still have questions, my prayer for you is that you will take the time to research this topic and find answers.

Unswervingly,

Derek Johnson

Hebrews 10:23
*Statistic taken from http://www.organdonor.gov/ and accessed on July 7, 2015
**Statistics were taken from http://www.life-source.org/ and accessed on July 7, 2015

Printed in the United States
By Bookmasters